A delightful poetic confection featuring Lawrence Ferlinghetti

and poems and art by 223 San Diego students.

BORDER VOICES /12

ISBN, BORDER VOICES
0-9719906-4-6

Jack Webb
P.O. Box 120191
San Diego, CA 92112-0191

Poet-painter Lawrence Ferlinghetti, along with some of the student poets featured
with him in this anthology, read poems at the 2005 Border Voices Poetry Fair.
The Fair was presented by the Associated Students of San Diego State University
and *The San Diego Union-Tribune*, in collaboration with
the Border Voices Poetry Project.

Art Director: Leslie L.J. Reilly
Lilac Design Studio

Editors: Chris Dickerson and Celia Sigmon

Introduction, and biography of Lawrence Ferlinghetti: Jack Webb

Photo of Lawrence Ferlinghetti by Steven C. Wilson

Cover Illustrations:
Starry City Night Life by Albert Ayson Jr. / Morse High School,
Look on the Bright Side by Jennifer Zamora / Marston Middle School

DEDICATION

This book is dedicated to the poets who teach in San Diego classrooms as part of the Border Voices Poetry Project. Both in their work with students, and in the beautiful results we see in this anthology of student poems, we find confirmation that

"Teaching is an act of love."

– Antonia Darder
professor of Educational Policy Studies
and Latino/a Studies at the University of
Illinois, Urbana Champaign

CONTENTS

Dedication   1
Introduction   9
Acknowledgements   21

LAWRENCE FERLINGHETTI
The beat goes on...   25

STUDENT POETS   29

Matthew Belden	*Haiku*	30
Danielle Nelson	*New York City Street Flowers*	31
Anna Ponting	*Dream Street, Pittsburgh, PA., 1956*	32
Bryant Diep	*Midnight Chill*	33
Geronimo Perez	*Dirty Streets*	34
Charlotte Stern	*Street Cats*	35
Lauren Boulger	*City of Confusion*	36
Devin Salemi	*Geometry and Jade*	37
Kristin Sammons	*Curiosity Keeps Calling*	38
Bridget Kilgallon	*Ballad of Pandora*	39
Frantz Farreau	*The Four Winds*	40-1
Kari Neal	*After Peter Brueghel's "The Fall of Icarus"*	42
Jack Meaney	*Titus' Lament*	43
Jesse Morgan Unger	*My Blood Turns Blue—*	44
	Hamlet to Gertrude	
Diana Chaudron	*Smiling Jack (The Ripper's Reflection)*	45
Wesley Hawkins	*Confessions of Bloodbeard the Pirate*	46
Morgan Lair	*Silverstein's Dream*	47
Angelica Bernabe	*Brazil*	48
Octavia Marks	*Classy Material*	49
Steve Bako	*Eyewitness*	50
Andrew Miller	*Wind*	51
Jacob Katz	*Poetry*	52

Alisa Inthavong	*I Come From a Land*	53
Edrees Nassir	*Afghani Volcano*	54
Mattie Conway	*The Drowning World*	55
Lilia Barrera	*Proud People*	56
Rachelle Joseph	*No Color*	57
Tommy Garber	*How to Run Away From Home Without Leaving Your Room*	58
Antigone Brickman	*In a Dream*	59
Kevin Farley	*My Dreams*	60
Tara Ash-Reynolds	*My Medicine Bag*	61
Reece Camper	*I Hate Poems*	62
Jake Euhus	*Blocks*	63
Kylee Danielson	*The Tender Emotions of Household Objects*	64-5
Justin Shephard	*Apple Face*	66
Nathan Tea	*Three Friends*	67
Emily Schreiber	*Before I Was a Tire*	68
Aubrey Bunday	*The Beach House*	69
Jeffrey Murray	*Cello*	70
Laura Yan	*Dancing on Steel Strings*	71
Michael Villanueva	*Ode to Bach*	72
Zaira Ramirez	*Silky Silence*	73
Rodrigo Flake	*Ms. Sax*	74
David Nguyen	*Midnight Music*	75
Mauricio Ovideo	*If I Were a Flute*	76
Stephanie Kuzara	*Song of Words*	77
Alisa Feinswog	*Colors*	78
Matthew Vollgraff	*The Ascension*	79
Emily Brynne Towry	*Depression*	80
Matthew Higgins	*Sorrowful Thoughts*	81
Adam Perez	*Survivor*	82
William Nakamura	*The Ending of Life*	83
Ya'Sin Ibn Idris	*Flowers*	84
Ryanne McNeill	*Listen*	85
Caleb Adkins	*The Island of Peace*	86
Esteban Ibarra	*Sea*	87
Cameron Koob	*Rock*	88
Kendra Petersen	*I Am My Own Rock*	89
Eber Valdovinos	*Smooth and Slithering*	90
Marika Vigo	*The Ugly Mask Magician*	91

Cori Saffel	*The Chat*	92
Amy Tran	*Amy the Alligator*	93
Allison Branch	*My House*	94
Alyssa Jenkins	*What a House Really Is*	95
Ernest Ciballos	*Eden*	96
Mauricio Bojorgez	*In Spring*	97
Anissa Navarro	*In The Wind of a Circle*	98
Alex Leatham	*The Trees' Cry*	99
Troy Rayder	*The Color of Fall*	100
Scott Glass	*The Fall Poem*	101
Nicholas McGee	*The Reaping*	102
Christa Watkins	*A Fall Day*	103
Sofia Raimondi	*Swedish Thanksgiving*	104
Claire Tompkins	*The Brown Leaf*	105
Qing Ping He	*Time Traveler*	106
Eric Ponce	*Amazing Desert*	107
Vanessa Peth	*Honey Snow*	108
Frank Poolev	*Winter*	109
Jose Hernandez III	*The Dream*	110
April Martinez	*The Wind's Fingers*	111
Kianna Eberle	*Screeches of Starlight*	112
Alex Castilla	*Shape Party*	113
Tania Sweis	*Ode to a Star*	114
Meghan O'Brien	*Ode to My Horse*	115
David Draskovich	*The Spider*	116
Taylor Madigan	*Black Widow*	117
Madelline Hohmann	*Because I Can't Find You in My Heart*	118
Gabriela Kramer	*Haiku*	119
Schuyler Lolly	*Moonlit Walk*	119

Nightfall by Anna Armitage / Marston Middle School

Elizabeth Nichols	*Black Tipped Dusk*	120
Nicholas Sanchez	*The Night Coyote*	121
Noah Resto	*Mystery Border*	122
Kylie Williams	*The Other Side*	123
Christopher Escobar	*Mystical Cholla*	124
Brianna Contreras	*Opal Sunrise*	125
Madeline Thunder	*A Gift (for my mom)*	126
Emmanuel Mercado	*Grandfather Lorenzo*	127
Rachel Nasland	*White*	128
Giovanni Rios	*School*	129
Jamielou Trajano	*Married to My Eraser*	130
Jessica Funk	*There's Time for Math Tomorrow*	131
Daniela Jinich	*Class*	132-3
Nick Sugihara	*Ode to my Shoes*	134
Adam Edward Trainor	*I Am Not a Shoe*	135
Esperanza DeLap	*My Rusty Cell*	136
Sara Connor	*Me*	137
Dorothy Manimtim	*Tatay*	138
Isabella Guiha	*Taunting the Suicidal*	139
Hailey Mashburn	*When Will People Notice Me?*	140
Yukino Strong	*The Scar of Chaos*	141
Eric Phillpott	*Modern Haiku*	142
Rayna Kilroy	*Closed Eyes, Open Mouths*	143
Chris McDaniel	*Problems*	144
Kyle Rigg	*War*	145
Bashir Wyatt	*Look at That Runner*	146
Weslie Hawkins	*What I am Aiming For*	147
Nuria Cruz	*The Words of Red*	148
Anna Najor	*Giving to You*	149
Lisett Peña	*La Novia*	150
Sarai Velazco	*The Heart Poem*	151
Alvin Balmeo	*My Perfect Pet*	152
Alison Tradonsky	*The Solid Dog with Lots of Friends*	153
Octavia Marks	*Family Portrait*	154
Carla Torres	*Mi Papá / My Father*	155
Jessica Rodriguez	*The Omen*	156
Morgan Heck	*My UCLA Helmet*	157
Pedro Cardenas	*Jackhammer Hands*	158
Kyle Ingraham	*Poetry's Actions*	159
Alejandra Ruiz	*Brown Scarred Hands*	160

Dani Shapiro	*My Father's Hands*	161
Rikki Jean Celiceo	*A Welder's Hands*	162
Silviano Valdez	*How to Paint Love*	163
Sarah Faxon	*Ballad of the Orphaned Boy*	164-5
Matthew Higgins	*Depressed (Dramatic Poem)*	166
Natalie Diebold	*What Do I Think of Poetry?*	167
Sarah LaBanc	*A Child*	168
Carlos Sanchez	*The Bones on the Floor*	169
Brian Tran	*Spaghetti*	170
Andrey Payne	*Sea of Writing*	171
Jake Rappoport	*How to Bake a Poem*	172
Jessica Strickland	*My Fork is Ready*	173
Chris Mancillas	*The Awakening*	174
Fernanda Lezama	*Key of Z Confusion*	175
Sarah Cheng	*Kitchen in China*	176
Giselle Luevano	*Like Gum Stuck to Your Shoe*	177
Mollie Friedlander	*Chamomile*	178
Luis Santos	*Red Cardinals in Summer*	179
Siobhan Matheson	*Banana Smoothie*	180
Tiffany Hernandez Diaz	*Tiffany the Tangerine Tiger*	181
Jimmy Nguyen	*The Freezer*	182
Nick M. Nasirpour	*Peace Poem*	183
Christine Kim	*The Ocean Inside Me*	184
Vanessa Chappins	*Blue Poetry*	185

HONORABLE MENTIONS 187-199

Lonely Stick by Ryan Gadiano / Morse High School

INTRODUCTION

By Jack Webb, Director

Border Voices Poetry Project

It's the little things that make the Border Voices Poetry Project worthwhile. Like the kiss a skinny 16-year-old girl in a beret planted on the silver-gray head of Lawrence Ferlinghetti on April 11, 1997. And the magic stone she handed him, with tears in her eyes, after listening to him recite poetry to the rhythms of a jazz band at the 4th annual Border Voices Poetry Fair.

"Oh, Mr. Ferlinghetti, you were so wonderful tonight," she said.

That memory is especially poignant this year, as we prepare for the 12th annual Poetry Fair on April 29, 2005, and I will return to it in a moment. But first, a bit of explanation, both about the fair and this book, as well as the appearance of Mr. Ferlinghetti in the first paragraph of this little essay.

Because of a series of emergencies – including a medical operation I had to undergo in late January – this year's fair was trimmed back. We had originally planned our usual stellar lineup of several poets, including N. Scott Momaday, W.S. Merwin, Kathleen Norris and Li-Young Lee in addition to Ferlinghetti in a return engagement. The contracts had been signed, initial preparations made.

We wanted the fair to be extra-special this year, because we had a lot to celebrate. We had won several prizes for our weekly Border Voices TV show, featuring the kids of San Diego interacting with famous poets from around the world. We'd won other prizes for promoting the arts and education in San Diego. Most important, our marvelous poet-teachers – a full list of whom can be found on our Web site, bordervoices.com – had received fresh confirmation that their work was having a real impact on San Diego kids and their families.

The series of emergencies meant we had to trim our fair lineup to one great poet, the inimitable Ferlinghetti. And as a result, we have only him headlining this book, rather than the five or six major poets and their poems usually featured in Border Voices anthologies.

But we DO have many poems, and many sketches and other bits of art, by young people who participated in Border Voices poetry workshops during the last year. And we still have many reasons to celebrate, not the least of which is the powerful impact poetry workshops have had on student test scores and self-esteem.

The following may be familiar to some readers. It is an updated version of the table that appeared in the introduction to last year's anthology. It records the astonishing results of introducing poetry workshops into every classroom at Pershing Middle School in Spring 2002, an experiment that resulted in what the principal described as a campuswide "educational Renaissance" and "huge and continuing increases in scores on standardized English tests." Most significantly, the latest results – for 2004 – show that the poetry-influenced improvement in student test scores has continued and accelerated:

All Pershing Students, Spring 2001-2004

Percentage of School's Students at Each Performance Level

English Language Arts

	Far Below Basic		Below Basic		Basic		Proficient		Advanced	
	#	%	#	%	#	%	#	%	#	%
2004	**44**	**4.9**	**135**	**14.9**	**323**	**35.7**	**271**	**30**	**131**	**14.5**
2003	84	8.7	132	13.7	320	33.3	305	31.7	120	12.5
2002	92	10.0	152	16.5	338	36.8	256	27.9	81	8.8
2001	93	10.0	151	16.2	352	37.7	259	27.8	78	8.4

I know that tables like the above are irretrievably boring to some, so I will try to enliven its appearance on this page with a bit of background and personal anecdote. In doing so, I will – hopefully – create a context in which the true and exciting significance of the table will gracefully reveal itself.

In late 2001, the volunteers in Border Voices were excited. We'd put together a long and detailed proposal for experimental poetry workshops at Pershing Middle School, and sent the plan off to the California Arts Council. In Fall 2001, we learned that our hours of brainstorming and number-crunching had been rewarded with a $20,000 grant. The volunteer administrators got to work, scheduling the poets to go into Pershing classrooms in Spring 2002 and coordinating plans with Pershing administrators. For my part, I arranged for the brilliantly humorous poet Gary Soto to fly in for a reading and pep talk at the school, got a film crew to videotape the experiment, and made plans to feature the project at subsequent Border Voices poetry fairs at San Diego State University.

This project was SPECIAL. Border Voices had been sending

poets into classrooms throughout San Diego County since 1993, and there had been plenty of anecdotal evidence that it had helped kids and teachers. We'd heard about members of youth gangs who'd quit the street life after being introduced to the self-validating art of poetry. We'd heard about gifted kids who'd been inspired to use their gifts because of the healthy pride engendered by the art of verse.

But, generally speaking, teachers could not afford to bring poets into any one classroom for more than a week at a time. Despite their knowledge that Border Voices workshops were helping their kids, teachers had to scrimp and save and beg for school site funds to hire a poet for their classroom. We were lucky if one poet a semester could visit a handful of classrooms at any one school.

The Pershing grant enabled us to put poets into every classroom at Pershing. The results were phenomenal.

Look back at the table. Note how the number of students performing at advanced levels increased from 8.4% of the student body before the workshops to 14.5% by 2004. Note a corresponding drop in those scoring far below basic. Sarah Sullivan, the school principal, attributes the continuing increases in scores, in part, to teachers adopting Border Voices methods of presenting creative writing. She also said the workshops resulted in a new collegiality among the faculty, which in turn engendered the campuswide educational Renaissance referred to above . . .

When kids or adults learn to use language well, through poetry, their pride in themselves grows. All good poets have, as one of their gifts, a healthy pride, and it is good for them and for the community.

We rejoice – for example – in the in-your-face, soaring pride of Walt Whitman, and part of that rejoicing comes from our empathy with his vaunting, unashamed glorying in himself:

> I celebrate myself, and sing myself,
> And what I assume you shall assume,
> For every atom belonging to me as good belongs to you . . .

We rejoice as well in the paradoxical pride of the reclusive Emily Dickinson, too delicate a pearl ever to leave her Amherst home except on the wings of her own mind, too strong-willed to say anything except exactly what she was thinking about and damn the poetic conventions, her sensitive artistic antennae filtering joyful insight out of her garden and conversations with a few friends:

> Inebriate of Air – am I –
> And Debauchee of Dew –
> Reeling – thro endless summer days –
> From inns of Molten Blue –
>
> When "Landlords" turn the drunken Bee
> Out of the Foxglove's door –
> When Butterflies – renounce their "drams" –
> I shall but drink the more!
>
> Till Seraphs swing their snowy Hats –
> And Saints – to windows run –
> To see the little Tippler
> Leaning against the – Sun –

We can rejoice, too, at the poems in this book, and what they mean for us and our kids. Listen, for example, to this year's first-place poem in the middle school division, which hammers us like the beating of a drum. Here is the first stanza, and the last:

> New York City street flowers
> tough and hard core street flowers
> combat boots on feet flowers
> New York City street flowers
>
> New York City street flowers
> opaque and unique flowers
> only one place to find such street flowers
> on the
> Shoe bitten
> Gum ridden
> Coin filled
> Blood spilled
> Dreams gained
> Untamed
> New York City Streets

> **— Danielle Nelson**
> Grade 8, Standley Middle
> Poet-Teacher: Glory Foster
> Teacher: Reissa Schrager-Cole

I ask you – for a moment – to put yourself in the mind of Danielle Nelson, as her poem invites us to do. There is humor here, and empathy, and a joy reflected in the heavy rhythms. It is an infectious joy, and such joy is healthy for all of us.

Back to 1997, where Ferlinghetti has just finished his reading at SDSU's Montezuma Hall.

A crowd of 1,100 had cheered, cried, shouted and clapped through the San Francisco's poet's fiercely brilliant performance. Then Ferlinghetti had gone to his dressing room to rest as jazz saxophonist Charles McPherson and his quintet concluded the first day of the annual Border Voices Fair with a 45-minute concert.

I escorted Ferlinghetti to his room, then returned to the main hall to find the ushers wrestling with a crisis. Standing shoulder to shoulder, they were holding back a mini-mob of gently insistent teenagers who were crowded around the entrance to the

Wings by Amron Lopez / Morse High School

15

dressing room area. One of the ushers caught my eye.

"I didn't think 78-year-old poets had groupies," he said.

"It looks like Ferlinghetti does," I said.

One of the teenagers waved at the usher frantically. "I have to see Mr. Ferlinghetti!" she said.

"No on is allowed in the dressing room," the usher said firmly.

"But I have something to give him," the teenager said. She was close to tears, her beret perched at a forlorn angle on her blonde curls.

"What do you want to give him?" I asked. She looked at me hopefully and extended her right hand, slowly unfurling her fingers to reveal a brightly polished stone.

"Is it a magical stone?" I asked. She just looked at me and said again, "I have to see Mr. Ferlinghetti."

The girl's determination impressed me.

"Let me ask him," I said.

The poet was sitting at a table in the dressing room, unwinding from what had been a powerful performance. In 30 minutes he would be sitting at a huge table in the main hall, autographing his books for hundreds of fans. I wasn't at all sure this contemporary of novelist Jack Kerouac and poet Allen Ginsberg – this much-honored and much-traveled icon of 20th Century literature – wanted to spend his "down" time talking to a young fan. But his reaction was instantaneous, his piercingly bright blue eyes lighting up as he said, "Sure, bring her in."

The teenager rushed ahead of me into Ferlinghetti's dressing room. She stopped and stared and was silent for a long moment.

"Oh, Mr. Ferlinghetti, you were so wonderful tonight," she finally said.

"Thank you," he said, smiling. Ferlinghetti is a quiet, gentle man when he's not performing, a man of very few words. A long-time friend of the poet told me his frequent silences are sometimes mistaken for lack of interest, or a sort of prophetic and distant reverie, when, in fact, he is "just a very shy man." On this special night, however, I could see him going out of his way to put the teenager at ease.

She showed him her stone.

"Mr. Ferlinghetti, I want to give you this. Two years ago, a Border Voices poet came into our classroom and gave each of us a stone, or a leaf, or something else to write about. I got this stone. I wrote my first poem about it, and now poetry is a big part of my life, and I just love your poetry and . . . well, I want you to have this."

Ferlinghetti took the stone and admired it. "I'll put it on the

Cheer Up by Brandon Luzano / Morse High School

shelf in my office," he said.

Then the teenager leaned down and kissed him on the top of his head.

"I love you," she said, and turned, tears in her eyes, and rushed from the room.

It was a wonderful moment, both for Ferlinghetti, and for those involved in Border Voices. For him, it was a chance to see

Love Connection: Opposites Attract by Jamielou Trajano / Morse High School

his poetry affecting the lives of a new generation. For the rest of us, it was proof, yet again, that Border Voices is working.

We can all be proud, of our kids and ourselves. And that's a healthy thing.

ACKNOWLEDGEMENTS

This book and the April 2005 Poetry Fair are the result of a collaboration between dozens of poets, teachers and organizations; special thanks go to those organizations and individuals who helped underwrite this book and the Fair. Among those who have supported Border Voices with both donations and encouragement over the years are the James S. Copley Foundation; the San Diego Commission for Arts and Culture; the John R. and Jane F. Adams Endowment; the California Arts Council; Deborah Szekely, president of the Eureka Communities foundation; the Fieldstone Foundation; Audrey Geisel of the Dr. Seuss Foundation; Poets & Writers, Inc; and the National Endowment for the Arts. A special debt is owed the coterie of volunteer administrators who kept everything running smoothly through hard work leavened with humor, and especially the members of the executive board – Chris Baron, who doubled as fair manager; David Clary; Veronica Cunningham; Sylvia Levinson; and Celia Sigmon, who co-edited the annual anthology with Chris Dickerson. Thanks also to the judges who selected the student art and poetry for this anthology: Cali Linfor, Sylvia Levinson, Chris Dickerson and Gretchen Sousa.

And a VERY special thanks to *The San Diego Union-Tribune* for agreeing to co-sponsor the project, and to publish student poems and artwork in the newspaper at the time of the fair. Members of the *Union-Tribune* staff have expended many hours on the project, and the following list is not exhaustive: David Clary, assistant news editor; Vincent DePalma, the ever-helpful and conscientious Community Relations representative; Leslie L.J. Reilly, the graphic artist who designed this book, the fair poster, and other odds and ends, astonishing everyone for yet another year with her brilliance and good humor; Drew Schlosberg, Community and Public Relations manager; Jack Webb, assistant news editor and founder-director of Border Voices; and Margo Raynes, who helped make the annual March mailing to hundreds of students go smoothly in a stellar collaborative effort with Sylvia Levinson. Finally, we would like to express our deep appreciation to Karin Winner, editor of the *Union-Tribune*, for her continuing support over the years.

We also offer our deep appreciation to the poets to whom this book is dedicated – the 15 men and women who are currently going into San Diego County classrooms to teach the art of verse:

Francisco Bustos; Brandon Cesmat; Veronica Cunningham; Gloria Foster; Steven Garber; minerva (Gail N. Hawkins); Georgette James; Paula Jones; Roxanne Young Kilbourne; Seretta Martin; Jim Milner; Jill Moses and Johnnierenee Nia Nelson, co-area coordinators for California Poets in the Schools; Celia Sigmon; and Gabriela Anaya Valdapeña.

Following is a list of others who have contributed money, in-kind contributions, or moral and/or logistical support to the Border Voices Poetry Project:

The Administrators Association of San Diego City Schools; Sandra Alcosser of the Master of Fine Arts Program in Creative Writing at San Diego State University; the Associated Students of San Diego State University; the Association of San Diego Educators of the Gifted; Barnes & Noble/Bookstar; Borders Books

& Music; California Poets in the Schools; the San Diego Chargers; the San Diego County Office of Education, with special thanks to Dr. Rudy M. Castruita, superintendent, and Richard A. Harrison; Beverly Cramb; Ellen Lopez; Kermeen Fristrom; the Greater San Diego Council of Teachers of English; the San Diego Padres; the vivacious and ever-helpful Susan Schiele, general book buyer and book event coordinator, SDSU Bookstore; and Dr. Catherine Yi-yu Cho Woo, Professor Emeritus, San Diego State University.

Thanks, too, to the San Diego Unified School District and its talented administrators and staff, including the Office of the Superintendent as well as Janet D. Delaney, director of the Community Relations department. We are grateful for the help of dozens of other administrators and teachers in the district, and will pick one to represent them all: Sarah Sullivan, principal of Pershing Middle School, who helped the Border Voices Poetry Project organize and document one of its most ambitious programs – a full year of poetry workshops at the school, involving every student; with follow-up monitoring of standardized testing through 2004. Sincere appreciation goes, as well, to the National School District and its staff, teachers and administrators for their many years of active involvement in the project.

Finally, publisher Jack Webb wishes to take this opportunity to thank Joan S., helpmate extraordinaire who nursed him before and after two operations (pacemaker and open-heart). She exhibited enduring patience as he became cranky under the surgical battering and even crankier in the immediate aftermath. He acknowledges his debt to her, which he can never repay, and he also wishes to express his deep gratitude to others listed here who stood by him during difficult times.

LAWRENCE FERLINGHETTI

The beat goes on...

Rays by Victoria Herzberger / Marston Middle School

DRAGON'S TEETH

A headless man is running
down the street
He is carrying his head
in his hands
A woman runs after him
She has his heart
in her hands
The bombs keep falling
sowing hate
And they keep running
down the streets
Not the same two people
but thousands of others & brothers
All running
from the bombs that keep falling
sowing pure hate

And for every bomb that's dropped
up spring a thousand Bin Ladens
a thousand new terrorists
Like dragon's teeth sown
From which armed warriors sprang up
Crying for blood

As the smart bombs sowing hate
Keep falling and falling and falling

Lawrence Ferlinghetti remains a prominent voice of the poetry movement that began in the 1950s with the explosively controversial poems of the Beat generation. His own youth can be seen, in retrospect, as a sometimes harsh but always challenging preparation for his future literary acclaim. Ferlinghetti's father died shortly before the future poet was born in 1919 in Yonkers, N.Y., while his mother had a breakdown and was institutionalized. As a result, Ferlinghetti spent his youth living with various relatives and friends from New York to France. Well-versed in literature and art, he earned his Bachelor's degree at the University of North Carolina, a Master's degree at Columbia University, and a Doctorate de l'Université de Paris (Sorbonne). In the early 1950s, he settled in San Francisco where he founded City Lights Bookstore, the country's first all-paperbound bookshop, as well as the City Lights publishing imprint.

City Lights influenced an entire generation of poets and readers in an era called the San Francisco Renaissance, and Ferlinghetti himself – who has been described as "the foremost chronicler of our time" – has continued to exert a powerful influence with his lyrical, outrageous, and frequently satiric verse. His poetry collection *A Coney Island of the Mind* (1958) continues to be the most popular poetry book in the United States. It has been translated into nine languages and there are nearly 1,000,000 copies in print.

The author of poetry, plays, fiction, art criticism and essays, Ferlinghetti has a dozen books currently in print, while his paintings have been shown at galleries around the world. His most recent books are *A Far Rockway of the Heart* (1997), *How to Paint Sunlight* (2001), and *Americus Book I* (2004) published by New Directions. He has won numerous literary prizes, as well as the American Civil Liberties Union's Earl Warren Civil Liberties Award, and he was elected to the prestigious American Academy of Arts and Letters.

STUDENT POETS

Look on the Bright Side by Jennifer Zamora / Marston Middle School

THE HUMAN CONDITION

Starry City Night Life
by Albert Ayson Jr. / Morse High School

HAIKU

Beautiful flowers
In the city Chicago
On the dirty ground

Matthew Belden
Grade 4, Miramar Ranch Elementary School
Poet-teacher: Gabriela Anaya Valdepeña
Teacher: Michelle Andrejczuk

New York City Street Flowers

New York City street flowers
tough and hard core street flowers
combat boots on feet flowers
New York City street flowers

Watch pedestrians cross the street flowers
hear their screams and weep flowers
never to jump and leap flowers
New York City street flowers

Sun is smog to street flowers
hard to find but cheap flowers
nothing to lose, none to cheat flowers
New York City street flowers

New York City street flowers
opaque and unique flowers
only one place to find such street flowers
on the
    Shoe bitten
       Gum ridden
          Coin filled
             Blood spilled
                Dreams gained
                   Untamed
               New York City Streets

Danielle Nelson
Grade 8, Standley Middle School
Poet-teacher: Glory Foster
Teacher: Reissa Schrager-Cole

DREAM STREET, PITTSBURGH, PA, 1956
after a photography by Eugene Smith

The rusty white sign
stands prominent in the road
and its inky black letters
twist into the word
DREAM.
Unfortunately, the car
on the road didn't
make it far enough
to Dream Street.
He turned too early.
Now, because he made
one wrong mistake,
he's pulled his
life over
onto the sidelines,
his only company
the pale, scarce
daisies scattered
across the overgrown shoulder.
The old mailbox,
lonely in the shadows,
the big, leafy bushes
protect Dream Street
from the howling, dark
wind, and the halo
of light contrasts against the dark,
black shadows.
Dream Street,
that rusty white sign
in the street.

Anna Ponting
Grade 7, Lewis Middle School
Poet-teacher: Jill Moses
Teacher: Chris Silvestri

Midnight Chill

Calm howls of wind
In frozen midnight
Street lights flickering
In dark skies
Cars are speeding
On slippery roads

Bryant Diep
Grade 6, Montgomery Academy
Poet-teacher: Roxanne Kilbourne
Teacher: V. C. Groves

Life in the City by Alberto Soria / Rose Elementary School

DIRTY STREETS

I come from dirty streets
violence / hustling / gang banging
people stealing stuff from your cars
stereos, license plates, hubcaps

drunk men and women
staggering through stench-stained streets
bums sleeping on freeways
frantic, frazzled people selling / buying drugs

I come from dirty streets
where kids learn how to hustle
how to survive

Geronimo Perez
Grade 7, Marston Middle School
Poet-teacher: Johnnierenee Nelson
Teacher: Matt Snow

Street Cats

At midnight, when the clock turns 12:00
The street cats come out to play, black as night
But white as snow. Their eyes, like stars in the sky,
Glisten as they stare. Their tongues are pink as roses
But as rough as the loss of somebody you love.

I try to find these mysterious animals, but I never do.
Once I thought I caught a glimpse of them,
But they are like the wind nobody sees
And can never catch.
This is their secret.

Charlotte Stern
Grade 5, Jerabek Elementary School
Poet-teacher: Celia Sigmon
Teacher: Kathie Lloyd

Accidental Cat by Stephen Grantello / Morse High School

CITY OF CONFUSION

This hectic landscape
    catches my mind,
The brilliant colors of neon signs
    swirl around me like a hurricane.
The soul of the city blushes with
    rosy-red signs and fades at night.
And as a periwinkle sky covers the city,
The confusion of the universe keeps
    dark shadows on me,
      like a thundercloud ready to burst.

Lauren Boulger
Grade 5, Pacific Beach Elementary School
Poet-teacher: Veronica Cunningham
Teacher: Dave Sandler

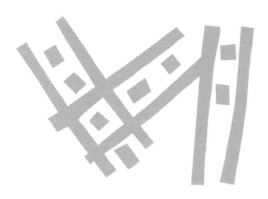

Lost by Tofa Faletufuga / Morse High School

GEOMETRY AND JADE
after "Green" by Magritte

A spatial paradox of green
fusing the organic and machine.
The moon shines bright
in a leaf of the universe
surrounded by time's triangle of lime.
Man shapes a unique perception of space
with humanity's array of color in time.
In an interconnecting matrix of geometry,
order is at hand, with entropy trapped in a box.

Devin Salemi
Grade 9, University City High School
Poet-teacher: Celia Sigmon
Teacher: Sally Owen

CURIOSITY KEEPS CALLING

Pandora,
she follows me around the house.
She whispers to me, to open the box.
Curiosity sometimes wears a disguise
a long, black, hooded cloak.

She tells me to look through the mail
or listen in on someone's phone call.
I always recognize her voice
a blend of cackle and snicker
and I try not to listen.

When you look at curiosity
she smiles, not an ordinary smile
but rather a smirk or a grin
as if she is up to something.
She usually is.

Kristin Sammons
Grade 7, Longfellow School
Poet-teacher: Johnnierenee Nelson
Teacher: Sarah Karp

BALLAD OF PANDORA

See Pandora sitting there
pretty dress of gold.
Same color as her long blonde hair,
eyes so blue and bold.

As a gift mighty Zeus created
a woman for the earth
From Hermes treachery, that she would be hated
most for giving birth.

Box in hand she was sent through a portal,
warned not to open the chest.
Alas, she was but a mere mortal,
curiosity got her best.

So late one night Pandora rose
and tiptoed to the crate.
And inside it she stuck her nose
releasing all the hate.

So now the world is full of sadness.
Evil was born that day.
Shrouded by chaos and madness,
forever here to stay.

Bridget Kilgallon
Grade 8, Marston Middle School
Poet-teacher: Gabriela Anaya Valdepeña
Teacher: Carol Matori

THE FOUR WINDS

Aelous, let loose your bagged winds
So they might do what they will.

If it be you, angry Boreas
Bring with you icy cold fury.
But do not forget your gentle snowflakes
That dance in the ballroom that is the sky.
Let them vest the soiled bride
In the purest white garment
So the groom might think for a moment
That his mate is not yet deflowered.

But if it be you, languid Notus
Lumber in with your heavy veil.
Make the girl the purest bride who knows
Not yet the state of matrimony.
Let the bride hide behind your veil,
Not seeing the world that surrounds her.
Hide her, oh hide her from the waiting groom
So that he may never lift the veil
To see the impure bride beneath.

And if it be you, gentle Zephyrus
Coax the groom out of his rage.
Reflower his fallen bride.
With your lulling voice remind him
Of his bride's sweet face and gentle touch.
Tell him it was he who deflowered her
In a sudden lover's passion
That knew no bounds.

But of you, sly Eurus
I know not what to ask,
For I know you are false.
Your gentle face and angel eyes
Do not hide that it is you who soiled the bride.
So stay away and do not try to fix
What you have cursed, for you know
It can never be undone.

Now Aeolus, let loose your winds
To tell the lover's tale.

Frantz Farreau
Grade 12, La Jolla High School
Poet-teacher: Gabriela Anaya Valdepeña
Teacher: Robin Visconti

Goddess of Darkness by Jasmine Vallejo / Mann Middle School

After Peter Brueghel's "The Fall of Icarus"

A flat, waxy painting lies upon my desk,
tiny recreation of a wondrous work of art.
And yet, in this small picture, a busy shoreline comes alive.
It draws me in and I can feel the sea's breath across my face.
The glorious sun beats down triumphant,
and the swaying sea digests a fallen man.
It is a calm serene escape, this picture—
though I question why I find beauty in it at all—
to know that below the quiet surface
a world comes alive and tells of a man
that rests now at the sea floor—
all because his dreams are too big for this world—
too big for this painting.

Kari Neal
Grade 12, La Jolla High School
Poet-teacher: Gabriela Anaya Valdepeña
Teacher: Robin Visconti

TITUS' LAMENT

Am I so base
that you, with stony gaze
can push away this flailing grasp,
and turn your back,
convict me to the void?
I strode with Mars and won great fame
and gave of mine
twenty and four to your father's war.
'Twas love, not haste
that let me make
them prey to Gothic blade.
And now my mind
corrupt with grief and rage
thirsts for blood.
Good Saturnine,
you that pull the shroud across my face,
in Hell shall rot
alone or together,
doubt me not.

Jack Meaney
Grade 12, La Jolla High School
Poet-teacher: Gabriela Anaya Valdepeña
Teacher: Robin Visconti

MY BLOOD TURNS BLUE—
HAMLET TO GERTRUDE

Suckling the bosom.
Kneeling at the breast.

Mother!
How damned am I?
    I have cursed you,
    Being me.
The second gravedigger throws dirt over his shoulder,
The third embalms our body,
The fourth is you.

Why I never loved you. . .
How shall I ever know?
I am criminal in my eyes, blasphemous in yours.
    My eyes see black.
    Yours see red.
We lived for the moment—but—
The moment is dead.

Oh, Mother: I do not seek your permission,
    I seek your revenge
        Like a cleaver through butter,
        The blade slides through my wrist.
        My blood turns blue
        For not loving you—
            How damned am I?

Jesse Morgan Unger
Grade 12, La Jolla High School
Poet-teacher: Gabriela Anaya Valdepeña
Teacher: Robin Visconti

SMILING JACK
(THE RIPPER'S REFLECTION)

As a child, I was ridiculed
For my deformity.
And now in my death,
I walk the streets of modern London,
A murderous specter.
If I returned,
I would host a macabre Mardi Gras
Celebrating my 300th anniversary.
They never discovered the face behind the masks.
And I, the consummate actor,
Excelled at creating illusion.
In the foggy East End
You can still trace my steps
On the slick cobblestone.
My reverie ended, but not by choice.
As I disappear
Into the mists of time,
Mockeries of myself
Still live on.
Copycats who paint in blood
Commemorate my legacy
Until they themselves are dust.

Diana Chaudron
Grade 9, University City High School
Poet-teacher: Celia Sigmon
Teacher: Sally Owen

CONFESSIONS OF BLOODBEARD THE PIRATE

Arrr, ye want ter hear 'bout me life, ye say?
I was a sailin' pirate, aye, o'er seas 'o gray.
Mighty battles I fought, niver lost a fight.
Except for one. T'was a terrible sight.

But before I tell yer 'ow I died,
Lemme tell ye 'bout me lighter side.
As a young'n, I went out 'n ran amuck,
Stealin' from shops 'n swipin' stuff.

Later in life, I found profit on the sea.
A real pirate, I was. I'd found me destiny!
But the things I miss most from me livin' days
Are me mateys, me grog, an' the piratin' ways.

Well, enough o' the rabble. This is 'ow I died:
We were fightin', when from the corner 'o my eye
I saw a seagull commin' at me. How fast he soared.
And BAM! He ran inta' me, and knocked me o'erboard!

If there's any advice I could give to ye,
Beware 'o birds. T'wer the death o' me!

Wesley Hawkins
Grade 9, University City High School
Poet-teacher: Celia Sigmon
Teacher: Sally Owen

SILVERSTEIN'S DREAM

Take a minute to stop and smell the apple blossoms.
Think of what you give and what you take,
And keep on looking for the wheel for your wedge
Or just go on rolling on your own.
What do I dream? Let me take one out of the freezer.
I'll warm it up, and you can put your feet in it, if you
    like.
I dream of absent doors and windows on a clubhouse,
Of stone airplanes and lost balloons.
Sometimes I get caught by the quick-digesting gink,
But I never get caught in its teeth.
I wish I could be back on my feet
Still looking for where the sidewalk ends
And trying to see the light in the darkness of the attic.
I might have met the little whale-eating girl
Who took 89 years to fulfill a promise,
Or Mrs. McTwitter, the babysitter,
Or even flown in a shoe with Ickle Me, Pickle Me
And Tickle Me, Too,
Fading into the distant sunset, chasing the wild
    strawberries,
Searching for the missing parts to my homework
    machine.
Maybe I'll buy a hula eel
From a Meehoo with an Exactlywatt in tow
Before tripping and falling up forever.
And if you are a dreamer, a wisher, a liar,
A hoper, a prayer, a magic-bean-buyer,
Come in, because you'll always be welcome
As the rose beneath these oaken boughs.

Morgan Lair
Grade 9, University City High School
Poet-teacher: Celia Sigmon
Teacher: Sally Owen

BRAZIL,

are you there? It's me, Angelica!
I haven't seen you in a long time. You are
my heart and soul, every time I think about
you, I start to cry. I feel so sad. Oh,
the happy carnival! *People laughing,*
and smiling and giggling. The beach so clear,
so blue, so warm, and clean. I miss you so
much and you don't even know it.
I am so proud to be part of you. You may have your
problems, but my people and I, especially,
think you are great. We were so happy,
I don't know why we left. We were happy and
didn't even know it. Do you still love me, Brazil?

Angelica Bernabe
Grade 8, Marston Middle School
Poet-teacher: Gabriela Anaya Valdepeña
Teacher: Kim Stinson

Shopping by April Joy Benito / Morse High School

CLASSY MATERIAL
inspired by "Open Shop" by Anton Van Dalen, 1980

Material Girl
white diamonds, a pizzazz of beauty, a glistening mane
  of golden hair
optical illusions surround her, offering more reflection
  to what is conspicuous
geometric queen-concentric circular patterns, jutting
angles and swirls of perfection
An inexplicable profoundness

Material Girl
egotistical, sophisticated
yet hidden in a shadowy mirror like a lost soul
  wandering
She does not realize the human within, the difficulty
  of challenging labor
She relies on outer beauty, improvident, taking the
  world for granted.

Material Girl
She'd rather dwell on ostentatious ensembles
jewels and sweet perfume
like a queen bee attracted to honey
than acknowledge the emptiness inside

So discombobulated with the value of life itself
Yet her extravagance
her seductive saunter
intrigues all who come her way.

Octavia Marks
Grade 10, Morse High School
Poet-teacher: Johnnierenee Nelson
Teacher: Carol Zupkas

EYEWITNESS

I was the lady in the corner picking a ripe fruit.
My thoughts were far away.
The man walked in and screamed.
I turned and looked him dead in the eye.
Then in a blink, I saw total darkness.

I was the man in the back
standing next to the lady in the corner.
A man came in and stood in the doorway, dripping wet.
I thought nothing of it at the time,
until I heard him shout and I was blasted back.
I hit the wall and couldn't get up.

I was across the street when that man walked into the store.
A few seconds later the store blew.
What was he thinking?
What made him do it?

Three dead and thirty-two wounded.
No one saw it coming.
No one knew why.

Steve Bako
Grade 9, Ramona High School
Poet-teacher: Seretta Martin
Teacher: Connie Mendoza

WIND

inspired by a photo of Marian Anderson
by Richard Avedon

I can see the wind
from the way her hair blows.
She does not notice
as her words are whipped away.
I can barely understand
but those she speaks to
do not need to understand.
She sings to her ancestors
and her words are carried away
across the wide flat plain,
eventually coming to rest
in the hearts of the ancient ones.

Andrew Miller
Grade 10, Morse High School
Poet-teacher: Glory Foster
Teacher: Cynthia Larkin

Power by Sherilyn Shamlow / Longfellow School

POETRY

Martin Luther King, Honest Abe, Rosa Parks—
people who saved the day

you think they are the nicest
people that ever were, but back then
people hated them.

They freed us all.

Jacob Katz
Grade 4, Miramar Elementary School
Poet-teacher: Gabriela Anaya Valdepeña
Teacher: Deborah Hartke

Nothing Can Hold Me Back
by Erick R. Melendez / Morse High School

I Come From a Land

full of water and rice
deep into religion
and respecting your elders.

I come from strict grandparents
who say that young girls should always
act lady-like and proper, respectful and quiet
never like the boys
whose voices are loud and vulgar.

I come from parents
who taught me the ways and traditions
of the people of their land,
going to temple on Sundays
celebrating Lao New Year.

I come from a people
who have worked hard
to gain all they have
from rice-farmers to maids
shop-keepers to seamstresses.

My language, my traditions
my personality, my growth
are a part of where I come from
a country so serene
with its old temples
and old ways.
A country called Laos.

Alisa Inthavong
Grade 10, Morse High School
Poet-teacher: Johnnierenee Nelson
Teacher: Jeff Meyer

AFGHANI VOLCANO

I come from Afghanistan.
I come from a country
where everyone worries about war.

A place where hunger
drought, sickness and death
is an everyday thing
like brushing your teeth.

A place where people
do not think about how
they look or what's in style
but how to make enough money
and if they'll survive until tomorrow.

Sometime I feel like an erupting volcano
burning everything in its path
angry at people's selfishness
a wildfire burning until nothing's left to burn
yet sometimes I feel calm
a stream on a sunny day.

My life is like a kaleidoscope
not knowing what color, shape, or size
the next picture will be.

Edrees Nassir
Grade 7, The Charter School of San Diego
Poet-teacher: Johnnierenee Nelson
Teacher: Samaiyah Vedder

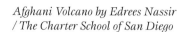

Afghani Volcano by Edrees Nassir
/ The Charter School of San Diego

THE DROWNING WORLD

I come from hope
waiting for the fire to burn
from grassy meadows
high mountains, dry lakes
and starving villages

We all want the fire to burn
yet we are embers under ash
shielding ourselves from the wind

Tradition is a drop of hope
within a rainstorm
memories drown
as time floats on
We are pulled weeds
with our roots still settled in the earth

Blind to history as it replays
before our eyes
we claw at empty space
always expecting equals to serve us
yet unwilling to serve

This is the drowning world
I come from
it has forgotten
the taste of air

Mattie Conway
Grade 7, Longfellow School
Poet-teacher: Johnnierenee Nelson
Teacher Sarah Karp

PROUD PEOPLE

I come from
the land of the ancient
Incas, Mayas, Aztecs
mathematicians
legendary laborers

I come from
the land of the Spanish
Cortez, Velasquez, Columbus
determined explorers
powerful conquistadors

I come from
great-grandparents
who lived one-hundred-plus years
who survived with only
tortillas, rice and beans

I come from
a people of genius
a people of might
a people who make me proud

Lilia Barrera
Grade 10, Morse High School
Poet-teacher: Johnnierenee Nelson
Teacher: Jeff Meyer

No Color

Being invisible means no color
  clear as a diamond
  invisible as a ghost.
Having no color means being empty.
But being human means
we can never run away
from our own color.

Rachelle Joseph
Grade 4, Jerabek Elementary School
Poet-Teacher: Celia Sigmon
Teacher: Kathy Comina

The Wrong Side of the Light
by Robert-Joseff E. Pelonia / Morse High School

THE ART OF LIVING

Sun Rising from the Night by Fauzia Maktabi / Morse High School

HOW TO RUN AWAY FROM HOME WITHOUT LEAVING YOUR ROOM

Find a spot, a small corner or nook.
Bring out a world that fits in
your palm, open its fresh, clean pages
cracking its ever-living spine.
Stare into its core, missing no detail.
Layer by layer, page by page.
Don't look away, even if your parents walk in.
Ignore everyone and everything.
Break through the skin of the fruit,
puncture the juicy inside.
Leave your room, your house,
    your world.

        Read.

Tommy Garber
Grade 6, Del Mar Heights Middle School
Poet-teacher: Jill Moses
Teacher: Kelly Johnson

IN A DREAM

A mystery, memory, gone in a flash,
only comes back in a dream.

Life, death, morning, night,
all the same in a dream

Lost in the rhythm of the canyon's rage,
that's what happens in a dream.

The power of the future and the weakness of the poor,
all seem strong in a dream.

Rage, hate, revenge, chaos,
all disappear in a dream.

Me, you, him, her,
all are one in a dream.

Antigone Brickman
Grade 4, Spreckels Elementary School
Poet-teacher: Jim Milner
Teacher: Peggy Araiza

MY DREAMS

My dreams are like a Porsche;
Strongly desired and elaborate
Fine details down to the most
Insignificant part.

My mind churns out thoughts
Like an engine churns horsepower.
It runs well at high speed, but
Gobbles energy at stop signs.

I obey no speed limit or
Traffic sign. My thoughts are
Compact, yet powerful.

Elegant yet simple.
Versatile but solid.
A simple shift in gears
Can change my thoughts.

I own my mind.
Own it like I own
The road. I obey no sign
No speed limit.

Kevin Farley
Grade 7, Lewis Middle School
Poet-teacher: Gabriela Anaya Valdepeña
Teacher: Chris Silvestri

My Medicine Bag

In a magical world, I am the problem solver
for animals and for people.
In my medicine bag, I have herbs to cure sickness,
rain that washes away problems,
a stick to knock you back to the real world,
the tooth of a shark to give you courage,
a blue jay's feather to help you
to see the light and not the dark,
a key to open up the door to freedom,
and a lightbulb to give you new ideas.
I would also use rain to wash away wars.
If someone was dying, I would use the feather
to help them see the beauty of life.
But in the real world, everyone has magic.
It is stored in the things you love.

Tara Ash-Reynolds
Grade 5, Jerabek Elementary School
Poet-teacher: Celia Sigmon
Teacher: Phyllis Porter

I HATE POEMS

Poems are stupid,
dumb and dry
like being inside
on a rainy day,
doing homework
while best friends play.
I'd rather be playing
or doing my chores,
or going with my mom
to the stores.
Either going out
or staying at home.
Anything's better than this
stupid poem.
So whatever you do,
please, read and enjoy.

Reece Camper
Grade 5, Hearst Elementary School
Poet-teacher: Jim Milner
Teacher: Chris Vasquez

BLOCKS

I've had these blocks since
I was two.
They had numbers and letters
written all over them.
It was fun while it lasted
but I still have the memory
inside my head
and inside the closet
where we left them then.
See, they smelled like wood,
felt smooth.
I see them as cubes
with no rust.
To hold them
I have a box
with my name imprinted.
You would hear nothing
from these little things
that taste like dust.

Jacob Euhus
Grade 3, San Pasqual Union School
Poet-teacher: Jim Milner
Teacher: Leah Hillus

THE TENDER EMOTIONS
OF HOUSEHOLD OBJECTS

Have you ever pondered the inner feelings of house-
hold objects?
Does my chair hug me
As I sit in it
Or does it long to push me into bed?
Outside, the garden whispers with questions.
Does the ground envy the sky
And wish that birds could fly
Among ITS rocks and pebbles?
Is the sticky sap of my tree a tear
or a trickle of laughter?
I walk back into the Darkness of the house.
I wonder
Is the pink kitchen always blushing
Because the white door is
Staring at her?
Breakfast comes like as storm
Bursting with smells.
Perhaps my orange juice is in love with carrots
or does it prefer sherbert?
The TV hummmms with the sound of cartoon rabbits
And the hunter who never makes his catch.
Is our TV WATCHING US and feeling sorry
or is it happy to be sucking up our lives?
It is time to shed the pajamas now
Like the wrinkled skin of a snake.
I wonder if my lovely old clothes are faithful
Like old friend
or do they GOSSIP in the closet?

Silly old shoes, are you happily married?
Or are you a divorced couple merely connected by the
  socks
you share?
Why is it that one sock is always missing?
Is it tired of being stepped on?
Will it remember the blushing kitchen,
The gossiping closet and the crying tree, or is it happy
  to be
lost?

Kylee Danielson
Grade 11, Heritage Christian School
Poet-teacher: Jill Moses
Teacher: Joyce Danielson

The Places We Go by Jennifer Lim / Morse High School

APPLE FACE
after "Son of Man" by Magritte

There's an apple as green as a parrot,
a bow tie as red as a ruby.
I see a turtle, whiter than a cloud
and a storm with no rain or lightning.
And those hats, black as midnight.
Never eat apples while its windy!

Justin Shephard
Grade 3, Flying Hills Elementary School
Poet-teacher: Celia Sigmon
Teacher: Anne Lindsay

Shadow by Blanca Rocha / Rose Elementary School

THREE FRIENDS

after "The Masterpiece" by Magritte

At the center I see three men
with skin as brown as dirt
and tree trunks and mud.
Their black derby hats
are as dark as midnight.
I see the sky, dark blue as dawn
with crescent moons
as white as starlight.
Three men can be friends.
Three moons can be friends, too.

Nathan Tea
Grade 3, Flying Hills Elementary School
Poet-teacher: Celia Sigmon
Teacher: Anne Lindsay

Before I Was a Tire

Before I was a tire,
I was a pile of used basketballs
Ready to be recycled.

Before I was a basketball,
I was a couple of hockey pucks
Ready to be melted down to rubber.

Before I was a hockey puck,
I was a few old piano keys
Ready to play a new tune in life.

Before I was a piano key,
I was a handful of pebbles
Ready to serve another master.

Before I was a pebble,
I was a pinch of sand
Ready to stop tumbling in the sand.

Before I was a grain of sand,
I was a neighborhood of dust
That accidentally fell into a piece of glue
And became a grain of sand.

Emily Schreiber
Grade 6, Heritage Christian School
Poet-teacher: Jill Moses
Teacher: Kim Schreiber

THE BEACH HOUSE
after "The Human Condition" by Magritte

At the center I see an easel
with the artist's painting
of a pretty blue sea,
blue as a blue whale,
and the sand as gold
as a golden retriever's fur.
The sky tastes like blue cotton candy
and the ball is as black
as a midnight sky.
Sometimes it's hard
to tell the difference
between what's real
and what's unreal.

Aubrey Bunday
Grade 3, Flying Hills Elementary School
Poet-teacher: Celia Sigmon
Teacher: Anne Lindsay

Cello

blanketing the earth with
black oceans and white streams
a soft melody, a tide in the vast
expanse of nothing
sprouting beauty from the gloom
raising life from the death
sharpened crests to supple hills
slowly, ever slowly
moving slowly over the plains
showing all the power of music

Jeffrey Murray
Grade 7, Lewis Middle School
Poet-teacher: Jill Moses
Teacher: Chris Silvestri

Make a Joyful Noise Unto the Lord
by Danielle S. Delossantos / Morse High School

DANCING ON STEEL STRINGS

Pink nails stained with glitter remain
Lines drawn like maps of the city
Pressing down on wood before silver frets
While the other moves to pick the strings
Her hands like fleas, jumping up and down
Or dragonflies landing on fresh green leaves
A swaying pattern, seeming the same
Creating music, that remains
A question floats to mind as I watch
Might hands recognize soft melodies?
They seem to answer with a flick
How they love to dance like stars
Figure skating, letting notes ring
Across the room, over the strings.

Laura Yan
Grade 8, Standley Middle School
Poet-teacher: Glory Foster
Teacher: Reissa Schrager-Cole

ODE TO BACH

As jagged as a knife, the violin stroke
Upbeat, excited, thunderous
Yet smooth as a cool ocean breeze
Calming the soul.
Compliments from the bass
As perfect harmony forms.
Young, spirited sounds flow through the air.
Climatic productions pierce the mind
Controlling the being of the audience.
Tempo changes enlighten spirits.
Imagination sparks
Purity reformed
The heart of music portrayed.

Michael Villanueva
Grade 8, Marston Middle School
Poet-teacher: Gabriela Anaya Valdepeña
Teacher: Carol Matori

SILKY SILENCE

Silence is a whistle with no twitter
a whisper with no words
a falcon flying through deep blue sky

Silence is a poinsettia floating on the wind
a dancer imitating a breeze
a dolphin swimming through silky water

Silence is a violin with no one to play it
a piano with no keys
a cheetah running on air

Zaira Ramirez
Grade 6, Otay Elementary School
Poet-teacher: Johnnierenee Nelson
Teacher: Raul Espino

Dance With Me! by Eunice P. Tingzon / Morse High School

Ms. Sax

WAAAA WAAAAHHH
she cries
as man twiddles her keys
forcing her to sing
a crimson love letter
to tickle ear drums
on a cold Thursday night
warming stone hearts
splashing color on greyscale
making happy birthdays
and spectacular blind dates
snapping fingers
tapping toes
bobbing heads
breaking the ice
breaking the monotony.

Rodrigo Flake
Grade 10, Morse High School
Poet-teacher: Johnnierenee Nelson
Teacher: Carol Zupkas

MIDNIGHT MUSIC

Jazz
an endless symphony of soul and emotion
sweet notes of music repeating
a wave of harmonious shooting stars
brighter than the glistening canary sun
mysterious as the pale midnight moon.

Who knew a brass trumpet, cold and hard
could make tones of joy and happiness?
The musician,
strong and tall
like the mightiest of mountains
reveals his true nature through his
soft magical fingers.

The cure for everything;
music is everywhere
music is eternal.
Music is life.

David Nguyen
Grade 10, Morse High School
Poet-teacher: Johnnierenee Nelson
Teacher: Carol Zupkas

One Life, One Love by David Nguyen / Morse High School

If I Were a Flute

If I were a flute
I would sound soft as silver
I would look like a one-tree forest
or a magical rain stick falling
from a cloud

Mauricio Ovideo
Grade 3, Euclid Elementary School
Poet-teacher: Johnnierenee Nelson
Teacher: Suzanne Hughes

I Love Music by Angelica Sturdevent / Morse High School

SONG OF WORDS

Writing is an everlasting song of three: a paper,
    a pencil, and me.
Each of an equal importance,
Each has a striking solo in the song.
The sheets of paper flutter open,
Quickly preparing themselves.
The old wooden pencil dances swiftly across the
    welcoming page.
I let my imagination loose,
My loyal pencil writing faster and faster like a stallion
    galloping over the earth.
This magnificent song sings by itself,
Twisting and turning gracefully through everlasting
    life,
Wrapping the beautiful song around me,
Making it my own.

Stephanie Kuzara
Grade 6, Marshall Middle School
Poet-teacher: Veronica Cunningham
Teacher: Deborah Whitehurst

The Beginning of the End
by Christian Smith / Morse High School

COLORS

A red tissue
after a boxing match

The relaxing orange sunset
after a long hard day

The yellow teeth of a poor man
after twenty years of not brushing

A brand new green garden hose
after using the old one

The bright blue sky
after a heavy rain

Purple as my bed as I drift
off to sleep

Alisa Feinswog
Grade 5, San Diego Jewish Academy
Poet-teacher: Jim Milner
Teacher: Cheryl Kolker

THE ASCENSION
a lobotomy

I am the echo rising from the embers of ages:
I embody a note
Held like a breath.
Inhaling the dance of dust,
Amidst the snarls of instruments and implements,
I see the steam pulsing from eternity
In the fog of an ether dream.

Then the conductor raises his scalpel

And severs endless centimeters of memory
And sifts this whole history through a burlap hourglass
And cuts every question into unasked answers.

I have not lost consciousness;
   it was   stolen from me.
Reading the runes of a past collapsed,
I will now know my memories by maps.

Matthew Vollgraff
Grade 12, La Jolla High School
Poet-teacher: Gabriela Anaya Valdepeña
Teacher: Robin Visconti

DEPRESSION

Depression knocks on my door
silent, with nothing to say.
She can't see in color
only in black and gray.
Confused, she can't explain
the way she feels.

She comes to me
dressed in fishnets
and a long dark dress.
It's hard to notice when she's left.
She comes and goes, never rests.

Depression can't smile.
She just sits
and stares at nothing
for a long while.
She tells me "Death is a midnight runner."

Emily Brynne Towry
Grade 10, The Charter School of San Diego
Poet-Teacher: Johnnierenee Nelson
Teacher: Sumaiyah Vedder

Afraid of Life by Vincente Lagajino / Morse High School

SORROWFUL THOUGHTS

Life is a sea of worry and lies, a bowl of sorrow and misery we must conquer. Life is a dream in our small little world. Why wonder why? We ought to be the smartest species, and yet we pollute. Some say there is no meaning no verisimilitude, we have no appearance. Isn't it all relative? We should live life to its fullest. We should worry about ourselves, our environment. Beauty is seen everywhere, but we only admire it in celebrities and not in the trees, the world around us. We ignore natural essence everywhere. We spend so much time on ourselves. We're all going to the same place. We have killed our aura, now we want more? We have baseless thoughts. Some try to replenish what we have destroyed, but we cannot fix our mistakes. There is no point. Try to set yourself free, our souls are all trapped, nowhere to run, nowhere to run—break away—run free.

Matthew Higgins
Grade 5, Santa Fe Montessori School
Poet-teacher: Gabriela Anaya Valdepeña
Teacher: Christine Beausoleil

SURVIVOR

Through the imaginary window I see a man.
Not your average man, but a man jumping off a cliff,
his hair blowing in the wind,
his mouth as frozen as ice,
his arms that look like they're broken.
But he survived the big action-packed fall.
This time of year there is no chance
I will ever see him again,
but I will always remember his hunkering face
in the winter of 2003. He is alive.

Adam Perez
Grade 3, Hearst Elementary School
Poet-teacher: Celia Sigmon
Teacher: Jean Feinstein

If Everyone Could Fly by Ryan Caganap / Morse High School

THE ENDING OF LIFE

1.
Meaning is everywhere and nowhere,
like a footprint at the beach,
left behind, its meaning gone;
it will soon be washed away
like a shadow, just following,
disappearing into darkness
when darkness comes.

2.
Many people eating,
many people talking,
some searching for a shady spot—
most have found one.
A summer day in the park.

3.
I see a door close,
another man or woman left
probably to return again,
or never to come,
to leave not only this café,
but perhaps this world,
to leave or to come,
each ends with a closing door,
a closing light,
an ending.

William Nakamura
Grade 5, Hearst Elementary School
Poet-teacher: Jim Milner
Teacher: Chris Vasquez

THE VOICES OF THE AIR

The World Paves a Path for Humankind
by Sharyn Ang / Morse High School

FLOWERS

Blooming yellow branches
Laughing through a waterfall
Smell like honey red roses
Growing in a summer field

Ya'Sin Ibn Idris
Grade 3, John Muir Alternative School
Poet-teacher: Roxanne Kilbourne
Teacher: Hope Grant

LISTEN

Listen with an open heart
to the periwinkle water falling.

Listen with an open mind
to the dark forgetting whispers
and the laughter of green leaves
as the wind tickles their tips.

Listen to the baby waves
as they hit the rocky shores.

Listen carefully to nature.
Let it help you.

Ryanne McNeill
Grade 4, Hearst Elementary School
Poet-teacher: Celia Sigmon
Teacher: Jean Feinstein

THE ISLAND OF PEACE
after "Dusk, 1908" by Monet

At the center I see an island.
There is a slight breeze
like the beginning of a new day.
I see tall thin rocks with the sun rays
as light yellow as the pale clouds,
the rocks bitten and chewed by the sea,
the foam as white as snow.
The island tells me that everything
about this life is peaceful and quiet.

Caleb Adkins
Grade 4, Flying Hills Elementary School
Poet-teacher: Celia Sigmon
Teacher: Marci Knoles

Euphoria Island by Kay Tiomico Langit /
Morse High School

SEA

Water and more water
I see a goldfish
at the surface, I see a sea otter.
Make a wish,
sour seaweed,
a gulping reed.
The whale sharks feed
at the bottom of a wheel.

Esteban Ibarra
Grade 4, Euclid Elementary School
Poet-teacher: Gabriela Anaya Valdepeña
Teacher: Shelley Woodruff

Rock

This one has traveled far
through sweet mountain mist and has
engraved dew in its coat. It has a
small mariachi band playing a brisk song.
It has the gift of a small crystal and has life in every
    corner.
Yet it poses age.

Cameron Koob
Grade 4, Ada Harris Elementary School
Poet-teacher: Jill Moses
Teacher: Trish D'Entremont

Mountains by David Alexander Keller / Otay Elementary School

I Am My Own Rock

I am my own rock,
the amazing color of sweet sand
on a promising beach.
I fit into a small dancing hand
of a blissful child.
I am trapped,
trapped in a pocket of laughter.
I whisper hope
through a soothing mind.
I rock the wild future
of fear!
As smooth as a calm river
of soulful music,
I shine like the magical moon
and the twinkling stars
on a dark promising night.
I am a singing rock
of wisdom.
I am my own rock.

Kendra Petersen
Grade 5, Dingeman Elementary School
Poet-teacher: Veronica Cunningham
Teacher: Rochelle Schwartz

SMOOTH AND SLITHERING

Its dark red
   eyes gleam
Its light
   brown skin
   Sheds in the
  blue night
    shade Its
   smooth scaly
     skin winding
    through the
   dark brown
   leaves Its
   body
  slithering
  up a tree
   in the pale
black night
Its mouth
with two
white
   milk teeth
Fangs
   to bite
you if you
disturb it
     Its tail
rattling
    Warning
you to
   get away

Eber Valdovinos
Grade 4, Rose Elementary School
Poet-teacher: Glory Foster
Teacher: Chuck Sullivant

THE UGLY MASK MAGICIAN

Look, my nose is a shark in the water!
See, my eyes look like bats. Listen, my hair
Looks like tons of tooth picks! Upside down my
Eyebrows look like two bent
Surf boards. Don't say I am a crab!
My mouth looks like a cave. My hat
Looks like a sponge! My name is shark game.

Marika Vigo
Grade 1, St. Patrick's School
Poet-teacher: Jill Moses
Teacher: Julie Rolefson

Serpent and the Shamrock by Daniel Leach / Morse High School

THE CHAT

I see a possum crying from loneliness.
I give him some Starbuck's coffee,
and we chat about life. He tells me
how he almost got eaten by an owl,
but he played dead and got away.
I tell him how I go to school. He tells me
how he once hung in a tree for two nights.
I tell him how I once slept for 15 hours.
His jaw drops. I wake up,
but a possum is on the window sill.
He does the can-can
and scurries into the bushes.

Cori Saffel
Grade 5, Jerabek Elementary School
Poet-teacher: Celia Sigmon
Teacher: Phyllis Porter

AMY THE ALLIGATOR

Amy the Alligator was
an artist who adored animals

apes and   a
    n
    t
      s

always attracted her attention.

Amy also enjoyed acting,

a   t
  c   a   i
   r   b   c
    o   s

and ACOUSTIC GUITAR.

Amy Tran
Grade 3, Euclid Elementary School
Poet-teacher: Johnnierenee Nelson
Teacher: Laura Brown

My House

The worn green walls
Flowers real and fake
Lining the windows.
The feeder
Filled with artificial nectar
Bringing hummingbirds to our garden.
Inside
The smell of dinner
Wafts in the living room.
My mother sitting on a couch
Watching the television
Drone on.
She sits with her glass of wine
A white-yellow color like blonde hair in the sun
All animals napping in the laziness
Of the evening.
Everything in the house is calm
Dead almost.
My eyes are dull with a feeling unexplainable.
I wait to fall asleep
Where maybe my dreams will bring
Some adventure and excitement.

Allison Branch
Grade 7, Lewis Middle School
Poet-teacher: Jill Moses
Teacher: Chris Silvestri

WHAT A HOUSE REALLY IS

Before you were a rickety old house you were
a young tree blossoming with flowers and youth.
And even before that you were a little scrawny
stick with branches and little buds of leaves.
Yet even before that you were a little sprout peeking
out of the earth to explore the world around you.
And then there was the beginning when you were
a seed wrapped in a soft, comforting blanket of earth.

Alyssa Jenkins
Grade 7, Heritage Christian School
Poet-teacher: Jill Moses
Teacher: Denise Jenkins

Good Night by Monica Hernandez / Rose Elementary School

EDEN

I miss tending my garden
the rice fields by the wayside
and how the sweltering heat died
when the cold night air drifted
into my ancient bones.

How I would watch
the patches of green
shimmer above still waters
under a glistening setting sun.
How I rejoiced
content with the work of my hands.

But here
the sun always shines
fire doesn't light the ground.
It blazes through clear
cloudless skies streaked
with brilliant blues.
Darkness descends upon the land
only to provide a shady comfort.

How I would watch
the pastures of endless green
the vast waters
an eternal abyss
under an everlasting, shining sun.

So, maybe, NO.
I don't miss tending my garden
for now I am part of one.
How I rejoice
content with the work of HIS hands.

Ernest Ciballos
Grade 10, Morse High School
Poet-teacher: Johnnierenee Nelson
Teacher: Jeff Meyer

IN SPRING
there are mariposas

In Spring
there are rosas rojas

In Spring
there are girasoles

In Primavera
there are squirrels.

Mauricio Bojorgez
Grade 3, Euclid Elementary School
Poet-teacher: Gabriela Anaya Valdepeña
Teacher: Susannah Saco

In the Wind of a Circle

I am the purple storm
Of summer
Running off on a friday
Roaring like a cheetah
In the wind of a circle
I am as monumental
As a giant redwood
In the ruby sky
I am as vivacious as a lion
Eating its prey on the ground
I am a soccer ball
Racing to score the winning goal
I am Splash Mountain
Going to Florida
I eat a red raspberry
On a wonderful day
In Paradise
I swim to the beach
On the sizzling black sand
Of Hawaii

Anissa Navarro
Grade 5, Rose Elementary School
Poet-teacher: Glory Foster
Teacher: Susan McKeon

THE TREES' CRY

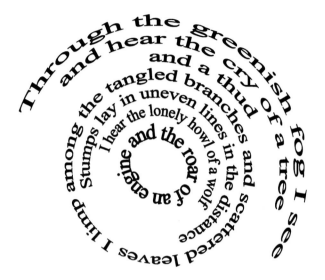

Through the greenish fog I see and hear the cry of a tree and a thud among the tangled branches and scattered Stumps lay in uneven lines in the distance I hear the lonely howl of a wolf and the roar of an engine as I limp

Alex Leatham
Grade 4, Ada Harris Elementary School
Poet-teacher: Brandon Cesmat
Teacher: Leslie Packard

THE COLOR OF FALL

I see the leaves on the trees
like gold and copper coins, gleaming in the sun.

I smell the tree's bark
as interesting as the smell of charcoal.

I taste the sweetness in the air
sweet as chocolate.

I hear the whistling wind
surfing across the aqua sky.

I touch the leaves, as crumbly and delicate
as warm cookies out of the oven.

I am the colors of Fall,
the gateway to the silver-white Winter.

Troy Rayder
Grade 5, Jerabek Elementary School
Poet-teacher: Celia Sigmon
Teacher: Phyllis Collins

THE FALL POEM

I am the colors of Fall.
I change the scarlet sun
to the silver moon.
I sing the great bear
into a great sleep.
I change the hot summer
into the silent cold winter.
I work day and night
plucking the leaves
to lay them down.
I work till I finish
and when Fall is done
I follow the sun.

Scott Glass
Grade 5, Jerabek Elementary School
Poet-teacher: Celia Sigmon
Teacher: Mary M. Wood

Egg Yolk Melting by Laura McCorkle / Marston Middle School

THE REAPING
after "Wheat Field Behind the Hospital" by Van Gogh

Midday sun on a shingled roof
Of the milling monolith,
Old Gaia's breath on cowhide panels.
Turn the wheels, grind the gears.
Down the path comes a mule
Laden with the wheat of years.
In the fields of golden waves,
Crimson walls and green brigades,
Humble men reap the bounty of their love.
Silver shining scythes slice down
The tender stocks of grain
Who, to the shining sun, stretch their necks
For a glimpse of open endless skies
Filled with nothing but the thoughts of clouds.
Their silent voices, lost in the vibrant fields,
Are never heard
But by a creaking lonely miller of winds.

Nicholas McGee
Grade 10, University City High School
Poet-teacher: Celia Sigmon
Teacher: Sally Owen

Looking Back by Ryan Saldaen / Morse High School

A Fall Day

Through the hayloft window
I see my grandfather driving his tractor
while my brother follows close behind
gathering leaves of crimson, gold and red.
I see my mother in the meadow
with her woven basket, picking berries
of all kinds, and my grandmother
making a pie by the window sill.
This time of year, there are no green leaves
except for the evergreens.
But I will always see the way
it seems as though there is a fire
glowing inside the leaves,
the way they crackle beneath me,
the way my brother pushes me
on the tire swing until I fall off
and roll in the embers of Fall.

Christa Watkins
Grade 4, Jerabek Elementary School
Poet-teacher: Celia Sigmon
Teachers: Jean Chalupsky and Angela Tucker

Swedish Thanksgiving

Through the invisible window I see deer
grazing while coyotes watch their prey,
turkeys trying to get out of reach of hungry hands,
the moon tiring out the sun to make it so cold.
This time of year, there are no light snowfalls,
the white heavens, no killer frostbite.
But I will always remember the moose
standing in the road while my car got closer, closer.
The brakes like screaming rattles
and the soft pit-pat of running hooves.

Sofia Raimondi
Grade 4, Jerabek Elementary School
Poet-teacher: Celia Sigmon
Teachers: Jean Chalupsky and Angela Tucker

THE BROWN LEAF

The brown leaf on the road
remembers the big oak tree.
The white snow drifts
getting larger. The
red, green, yellow, orange, and other
brown leaves, slowly drifting down.

I want you to see the
leaf, not a bright cheerful leaf,
but the brown leaf slowly
moving with the others
in the wind.

When you pick up the brown leaf,
take it home,
trace it,
make it more beautiful.

Claire Tompkins
Grade 4, Ada Harris Elementary School
Poet-teacher: Brandon Cesmat
Teacher: Trish D'Entremont

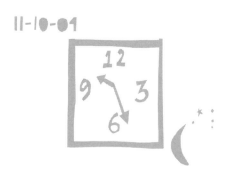

This Moment in Time
by Jennifer Leigh Keith Gozum / Morse High School

TIME TRAVELER

I am a dull,
freckled granite rock
with a jagged edge.
I, rock of twinkling steel gray granite
traveled slowly through time.
I remember that one day
I was lifted by fiery sand
and witnessed
many dinosaurs
dying
of a great
steaming
meteor.

Qing Ping He
Grade 4, Doyle Elementary School
Poet-teacher: Veronica Cunningham
Teacher: June Pecchia

Amazing Desert

inspired by "Saguaros At Sunset"
by Maynard Dixon

I want to show you the cactus
standing in the lonely desert.

I want to show you lizards
blending into copper colored rocks.

I want to show you a beautiful plain desert
filled with reptiles, bare brown trees.

I want to show you a divine sunset
the color of blood oranges.

I want to show you bright stars
and the full moon at night.

Eric Ponce
Grade 4, Otay Elementary School
Poet-teacher: Johnnierenee Nelson
Teacher: Carola Pandeli

HONEY SNOW

If I were a sunflower
I would smell like honey

If I were a parrot
I would sing to you

If I were snow
I would taste like chocolate
I would melt in your smooth hands

Vanessa Peth
Grade 3, Euclid Elementary School
Poet-Teacher: Johnnierenee Nelson
Teacher: Suzanne Hughes

My Wonderful Christmas Eve by Marilord Reyes / Morse High School

WINTER

after "Road With Cypress and Stars"
by Van Gogh

A little town
amongst the emerald hills
under a light blue sky
overlooks a farmer's fields.
The farmer is serious
while he cuts his wheat.
When he is done
the sky turns dark
the wind blows
a tree rocks
a door creeks.
The farmer looks up.
There is snow.

Frank Poole V
Grade 5, Jerabek Elementary School
Poet-teacher: Celia Sigmon
Teacher: Mary M. Wood

THE DREAM

The explosion
In my dream
Was like a frozen ice flicker
In the sky
Calling spring to the world
In winter.

Jose Hernandez III
Grade 3, John Muir Alternative School
Poet-teacher: Roxanne Kilbourne
Teacher: Hope Grant

THE WIND'S FINGERS

His soft blue black hair
Blew through the midnight sky
Silky ribbons
Lost
Wandering
On a starry night
With full crater Moon
The wind running her fingers through his hair

April Martinez
Grade 9, John Muir Alternative School
Poet-teacher: Roxanne Kilbourne
Teacher: Erin Kempf

Midnight by Sean M. Smith / Mann Middle School

Be a Star by My Dung Nguyen / Mann Middle School

Screeches of Starlight

The attack of darkness settles,
an enchanted glowing sphere
long over the horizon.
A blanket of evening draped over my world
for what seems like a decade.
It is the moonless night I beg to be freed from,
the blood-chilling winds.
Screeches of starlight lift my spirits.
My body flows without sense.

Kianna Eberle
Grade 5, Ada Harris Elementary School
Poet-teacher: Gabriela Anaya Valdepeña
Teacher: Sue Yant

SHAPE PARTY

after "Movement I" by Kandinsky

There's a party for the stars
that all takes place on the dark moons
    with streamers floating on different lines
    and shapes that look like staffs for music
    and polkadots dancing through the night.
The black background is dark as midnight
where the moons are hiding
    with small green and magenta flowers
    and rectangles and circles,
    points and corners and curves
    and other cool shapes.
The party never ends. It never ends.

Alex Castilla
Grade 4, Jerabek Elementary School
Poet-teacher: Celia Sigmon
Teacher: Tammy McDaniel

ODE TO A STAR

shining
glowing
a droplet of white paint
upon a pitch black canvas
brighter than a child's face
as he receives his birthday gifts
higher than an ant feels
atop an enormous tree
more beautiful
than a butterfly
resting its wings on a petal
it is
a firework,
set off by the moon
a luminous bird,
which flew too high,
a firefly
which got stuck in the sky
a reminder from the heavens
of the beauty of the Earth
it is
a star

Tania Sweis
Grade 7, Lewis Middle School
Poet-teacher: Jill Moses
Teacher: Chris Silvestri

My Pegasus by Kristalyn Obtera / Morse High School

ODE TO MY HORSE

She is a streak of lightning
across the night sky.
Her whinny is like
the crisp, cool
Autumn breeze.
She is the color
of desert sand.
Like a summer afternoon,
she is warm, round,
soft, and gentle.
But, she can be as fiery
as a cold winter night.
She bares the mark of speed
on her heel,
a white speck.
And the sign of friendship on her forehead,
a star.

Meghan O'Brien
Grade 6, Heritage Christian School
Poet-teacher: Jill Moses
Teacher: Laurie O'Brien

THE SPIDER

The black spider is the dark side of the moon.
It's as hairy as your grandmother's legs.
It yells for bugs the size of kingdom come,
and his web can stop time forever.

David Draskovich
Grade 3, Jerabek Elementary School
Poet-Teacher: Celia Sigmon
Teacher: Christy Martin

Broken Sun by Heather Dubrosky / Marston Middle School

BLACK WIDOW

The night is like a spider
casting its silky web across the sky.
The black spider wraps itself
around its prey
like the black coat of night
wrapping itself around the sky,
sucking the life from its prey
like the night sucking
the light from the world.
If the spider sees you
it scuddles behind a bush
like the night that dashes
behind the mountains
before the coming day.

Taylor Madigan
Grade 5, Jerabek Elementary School
Poet-teacher: Celia Sigmon
Teacher: Mary M. Wood

Because I Can't Find You in My Heart

Because your secret still remains
Because there's no one to turn to
Because you live
I go looking for you in the shadow of death
Beyond the enchantment
And find you lying in the grass
With a melody in the air.

Madelline Hohmann
Grade 8, Marston Middle School
Poet-teacher: Gabriela Anaya Valdepeña
Teacher: Mehrak Selby

Moonlit Walk

The rice fields are tamed
Cool night has come
To the cobbled stones

The crickets sing
Their starry melody
To harvesters at evening

Wind and moon
Ancient friends of night

Schuyler Lolly
Grade 12, La Jolla High School
Poet-teacher: Gabriela Anaya Valdepeña
Teacher: Robin Visconti

Haiku

As the sun's fading,
As darkness fills the soft moon—
I think of just you.

Gabriela Kramer
Grade 4, Miramar Ranch Elementary School
Poet-teacher: Gabriela Anaya Valdepeña
Teacher: Brian Vernia

BLACK TIPPED DUSK

The crow is like a dark, summer night
It flies SMACK into the window of morning.
I can hear it cawing as the sun warms its face
And forces its retreat into the west.
I feel the warmth on my face, and the chill at my back.
The crow grumbles in its throat as it tastes the
  bitterness of defeat.
Yet, he sees the same defeat every dawn,
And conquers every dusk.
But the smell of defeat is heady in its nostrils.
It smells the way nails on a chalkboard hear,
Bitter, and sour, and decayed in its mouth.
He is driven back, and back, past trees, and valleys
And piles of smoke anchored to small villages.
Crow becomes cheerful as he sees his dark feathers
Blanketing another part, the other part, of the world.
His crude laughter sprinkles China with dusk.
The dark midnight feathers drive back all thoughts of
  day,
As the dusk dissolves into points of stars.
The moon rubs her eyes, and sulkily peers at earth over
  her shoulder.
Even as the warm darkness floods on and on in rushing
  black tipped dusk.

Elizabeth Nichols
Grade 10, Heritage Christian School
Poet-teacher: Jill Moses
Teacher: Katherine Nichols

THE NIGHT COYOTE

The night is a coyote, as quiet as outer space.
Its eyes shine like the stars.
Its nose is dark as the shadows
poking into the kitchen corners.
When I see the coyote
it flees as swiftly as the blue wind.
It jumps to the moon, as high as heaven.
I am sad. I want to join coyote on the moon.
But he tells me I am just a human.

And I say humans have the power
to make dreams come true.

Nicholas Sanchez
Grade 5, Jerabek Elementary School
Poet-Teacher: Celia Sigmon
Teacher: Kathie Lloyd

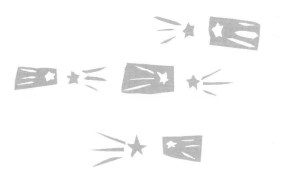

Shooting for the Stars by Nancy Quach / Marston Middle School

Space by Chynna Aloot Obana / Morse High School

MYSTERY BORDER

As wet graves border
The dead
From the beautiful living forever
Sugar matches the salty water
That takes away sadness for eternity.
Then yellow and gold petals
Of marigold flowers
Guide departed Spirits
To the singing stars.

Noah Resto
Grade 7, Bernardo Heights Middle School
Poet-teacher: Veronica Cunningham
Teacher: Karen McKenzie

THE OTHER SIDE

As the wavelets form the figured swell,
The sun falls from the sky.
The abandoned ship will never tell
Why the wave's filament embers die.

Some think it's paradise,
Others may diverge.
The tint of spice is shaded sapphire
When the sun and moon emerge.

Kylie Williams
Grade 7, Lewis Middle School
Poet-teacher: Gabriela Anaya Valdepeña
Teacher: Chris Silvestri

Mystical Cholla

I hold a cholla
against the sun and watch
as the sunlight glimmers through it
just as if it were a window.
If you look through one end
to the other you will see
it is a dusty telescope.
Hold it up at night
against the moon and
it will turn into a space shuttle
as the moonlight shines
against the tip of its wing.
You'll also see it is a flying star
dashing through the sky
and a miniature Saguaro cactus
or a curved magical time tunnel.
The cholla skeleton.

Christopher Escobar
Grade 5, Rose Elementary School
Poet-teacher: Glory Foster
Teacher: Carrie Cox

OPAL SUNRISE

Something about orange
is like the canyon view from my window
the morning sun, a gleaming burst that says "Hello."
Something about orange
is like the opal stone on my necklace.
It's like summer birds soaring free
across the meadow
for one last taste of the sweet tangerine breeze.
Something about orange
is like my mom's smile when she sees the sky.
Something about orange
is me.

Brianna Contreras
Grade 6, Montgomery Academy School
Poet-teacher: Roxanne Kilbourne
Teacher: V. C. Groves

A Dark Dark World by Shawn Bowman / Rose Elementary School

A GIFT (FOR MY MOM)

I give you the silver moon to shine light into your
dreams
and to keep you safe at night. I give you grace to seep
into your soul and your heart. I give you bright
colors to fill your world with joy and happiness.
I give you a flashlight so you can be a shining star of
your own.
I want to give you the seas, and mountains, and forests,
and jungles of the world.
I give you the first star of the night so it will shine
the way to the next part of the journey of your life.
I want to give you a glass full of faith
to bring you the courage you need.
I want to give you my heart and
all the love and tenderness I ever owned.
I want to give you life so you'll live
as long as the earth itself.
I give you these gifts so I will never lose you, Mom.

Madeline Thunder
Grade 4, Ada Harris Elementary School
Poet-teacher: Jill Moses
Teacher: Janice Murray

Starry Night by Jaimee Ngo / Morse High School

GRANDFATHER LORENZO

My grandfather is like a star
as far away as TJ.
I will always remember that cowboy hat
with a feather like a rainbow
after rain from the big blue sky
and all those funny jokes.
He teaches me that love
can not keep us apart
like borders and countries.

Emmanuel Mercado
Grade 4, Flying Hills Elementary School
Poet-Teacher: Celia Sigmon
Teacher: Marci Knoles

RITES OF PASSAGE

Moon & Sun by Sally Hoang / Mann Middle School

WHITE

I have many favorite colors,
but white is a color I can't stand.
It makes me feel empty and down
like I don't belong anywhere.
I don't mind wearing white.
It's just a simple color
when I'm a complicated girl.

Rachel Nasland
Grade 4, Jerabek Elementary School
Poet-teacher: Celia Sigmon
Teacher: Alison Knight

SCHOOL

At nine o'clock we
studied history,
but what we
learned is still
a mystery.
By ten, the class
moved on to math,
and waited for
the aftermath.
That was followed
  by
biology. We fell asleep
without apology.
English was what
next we studied
and our brains turned into silly
putty, 'till at last, the
lunch bell rang . . .
  we woke!
  we spoke!
  we ran!
  we sang!

Giovanni Rios
Grade 8, Marston Middle School
Poet-teacher: Gabriela Anaya Valdepeña
Teacher: Danielle Castagnola

MARRIED TO MY ERASER

Take away my faults
take away my dreams
What do you do?
Perfect or protect?

Take away my wrongs
take away my rights
how with each
back and forth motion
the constant struggle
of word leaving paper
everything disappears
    It's blank again
    It's blank again

Take away something good
Oh Eraser, it's your error
    this time around

You're nothing
You're everything
Let's face it
I need you

Take away a line I just wrote
take away my sanity

Look, I'm praising an eraser
a dirty, torn eraser!

Let's forget I even wrote about you
Erase this!

Jamielou Trajano
Grade 11, Morse High School
Poet-teacher: Johnnierenee Nelson
Teacher: Jeff Meyer

There's Time for Math Tomorrow

Yesterday I said
"I'll do my math project tomorrow"
Tomorrow is today
I need to:
research the origin
of triangles
calculate the weight
of a feather
draw pie charts
of government funds
discover
the 5th dimension
never mind
I don't know the 4th
Use the Quadratic Equation
to carefully measure
how long time travel takes
and while I'm at it
I need to cube root
a cube disguised as a rectangle
measure the length
of my middle name
in centimeters
millimeters and decimeters
compute the circumference
of my milk glass
write the next
distance/time formula
and much more
I will do it
Like I said...Tomorrow...

Jessica Funk
Grade 8, Standley Middle School
Poet-teacher: Glory Foster
Teacher: Caitlin Cray

CLASS

In a classroom
in a school
we sat
on our table
and heard the teacher
we heard
not listening
sandwiches
fruits
in the air
hungrily
writing on
and on and on
wanting recess
5 minutes more
felt like 2,000
years
Algebra, Grammar
my head
messed up
like a chunk
of people
smushed
I was
sweating
hot like a desert
boys all around
my best friend
other side
of the big classroom
teachers talking
on and on and on

passing notes
was everything
teachers not
noticing
we were laughing
we were desperate
we were in the air
the teacher talking
on and on and on
it was boring
it was falling
asleep

Daniela Jinich
Grade 5, San Diego Jewish Academy
Poet-teacher: Jim Milner
Teacher: Cheryl Kolker

Boredom by Hazel Cruz / Morse High School

ODE TO MY SHOES

My shoes are like stones in a river
hopping, skipping, running, jumping
like black knights battling the dirt
and grime that rises.
The foundation of a skyscraper.
The building blocks of my beginning.
Couriers of the ground sending messages to my body.
They speak of trials and tribulations
from the hill that once was climbed.
They are the silver chariot of movement
the compass of my legs
dodging in and out, in and out
keeping to themselves
worn and tired
battle hardened
begging for a breath
a new and young successor.

Nick Sugihara
Grade 6, Del Mar Heights Middle School
Poet-teacher: Jill Moses
Teacher: Kelly Johnson

I Am Not a Shoe

I am not a shoe
I don't squeak
or drag on the ground
I don't stomp on the grassy surface
of the community park

I am not a shoe
I don't have long laces
waiting to be tied into neat little bows
I am not a high heel
clicking on the cement going to a fancy dance

I am not a shoe
I don't shelter the foot and toes
from the dirty puddles after a long rain storm
I do not befriend the sock

I am not a shoe
I don't have a goofy tongue
sticking out of the laces
I am not a slipper
with fuzzy, pink feathers on me

I am not a shoe

Adam Edward Trainor
Grade 8, Standley Middle School
Poet-teacher: Glory Foster
Teacher: Reissa Schrager-Cole

MY RUSTY CELL

I pace in my rusty cell.
The world is shut off.
I find nothing attractive.
The mush nuns brought was tasteless.
The birds' song is soundless.
The furniture is as restless as I
in my ruin atop a cloud.
Not a file to be seen to free myself
from this disease.
I desire nothingness.
The world is a ghostly, gloomy hour.
The crisp air is for grieving.
When will I see her merry-pink face frowning
asking me what took so long?
Let the last hour strike while I lie
on the cold, hard stone.

Esperanza DeLap
Grade 4, Miramar Ranch Elementary School
Poet-teacher: Gabriela Anaya Valdpepeña
Teacher: Michelle Andrejczuk

ME

I'm a loner, deep but strange
I am "gothic," fun and deranged
I am scary, loud and happy
I am mean, funny and sappy
No emotion, feelings of all sorts
Contradiction, that's me in short

A running Panther, kitten with snow white feet
Cold and dead, full heart-beat
Raging fire, cold winter snow
Endless maze, read me like a book from head to toe
Deep dark red, black and green
All the colors in between
A waterfall to raging rapids, cool calm lake
I am so real and yet so fake
Left and Right
Day and Night
Two people in one, both not the same,
I am so wild and yet so tame

Sara Connor
Grade 8, Standley Middle School
Poet-teacher: Glory Foster
Teacher: Caitlin Cray

Dark by Arjie-Abigail Lopez / Morse High School

Tatay

Anak
as much as I would like to
I can't go back
and guide you
I can't argue
with your mommy anymore
on your behalf
like when you
cut your hair
with scissors.

Yet
I do not wish to return
to my decrepit body
of hollow bone casing
exhausted muscle
and sinew
for it no longer
belongs to me
but to the grass
the soil
the trees.

Nonetheless
I still wish
to watch you grow

Yet
the grass
the soil
the trees
do not permit
and that I regret.

Dorothy Manimtim
Grade 10, Morse High School
Poet-teacher: Johnnierenee Nelson
Teacher: Jeff Meyer

Taunting the Suicidal

Life hurts less when you're not alive
So go ahead and quit.
Suicide, always your empty threat
It's lost its meaning, so you may as well just act.
You said you wanted your ashes in the sea
Something about waves of time and poetry.
For all your false art,
I may as well put you in the backyard
Between the lawn gnome and the grave of my old rat
Or forgotten on the mantle
Beside the porcelain that likes to play Chinese.
I might even shed a mythical tear
So the devil and I can laugh about our inside jokes
   for eternity.
You prattled on
About being Heaven's slave
Or was it lord of Hell?
But none of that matters now
All you ever seem to make is Purgatory.

Isabella Guiha
Grade 12, La Jolla High School
Poet-teacher: Gabriela Anaya Valdepeña
Teacher: Robin Visconti

Ebony and Ivory by Czarina Galac / Morse High School

When Will People Notice Me?

I believe one cold, beautiful spring day,
I'll fall from my still position,
shining boldly once more
at the river's curving edge.
A smooth mountain rock,
locked inside a hollow willow tree.

I remember the cold river water in early spring,
but lose hope of returning.
Why have I been ignored
as my smooth marble edges
slowly turn to ancient fragments
of what I used to be?

Because as time moves on, rocks become old dust,
and nobody cares about
obsolete dust.

Hailey Mashburn
Grade 4, Sunset View Elementary School
Poet-teacher: Veronica Cunningham
Teacher: Rebecca Reid

Confused by Stephen Kelly / Morse High School

THE SCAR OF CHAOS

Do the delicate wings of art respect death?
Does the edge of a lonely heart soar with peace and
  freedom
or is it in fear of hopeless danger?
Are eyes the only window to an emotional soul?
Is the rushing river of youth hopeful or chaotic?
Is life the dark door to death?
How can you grow many eternal years, in one wary
  hour?
Why does music dance over many heads, but enter few
  open hearts?
Who holds betrayal in their fist, and who holds lost
  humor?

Yukino Strong
Grade 4, Hawthorne Elementary School
Poet-teacher: Veronica Cunningham
Teacher: Lana Sherman

Modern Haiku

Bullet the desert
Dictator hides in a hole
Iraq, bombed bald

Eric Phillpott
Grade 5, Miramar Ranch Elementary School
Poet-teacher: Gabriela Anaya Valdepeña
Teacher: Deborah Hartke

Operation Freedom by Tiffany Geronimo / Morse High School

CLOSED EYES, OPEN MOUTHS

I come from a land of locked doors
where security is what matters
where I can't walk my dog after sunset.

I come from a culture
which has lost all sense of culture
where every night televisions blare
atrocities in Iraq.

I come from a street
where mothers weep, fathers leave
where kids suffer slamming doors
and mothers' cooking has been replaced by TV dinners.

I come from a country of economic disaster.
We are used to cashing welfare checks.
Driving around a gunshot victim is uniform.
We are used to being forgotten.

I come from the reality of small paychecks.
We work all day, cry all night
while our pasts haunt us.
We think about it all.
We remember family dinners
sleeping with our windows open
staying out safely until nine.
We remember the descent into post-modernity.

I come from the greatest country in the world
AMERICA; this is my culture;
our newspapers are in the trash.

Rayna Kilroy
Grade 10, Morse High School
Poet-teacher: Johnnierenee Nelson
Teacher: Jeff Meyer

PROBLEMS

I never thought about the problems
Here in the USA
I never thought about the problems
In our country today.
All of my anger
Was toward the Middle East
When it's the USA who is the real beast.

Why won't Iraq cooperate with us?
Why are the citizens, making such a fuss?
All we want to do is rebuild a nation
And the only way to do so is by infiltration.

The President's actions are in need of revision
Like all of the abuse at the Abu-Ghraib prison.
What we need to do to rebuild Iraq
Is stop all the violence and bring our troops back.

I really can't believe what an absolute failure
Everybody is who voted for Nader.
He is the reason that peace has to wait
Taking votes from the Democratic Candidate.

So, before we're in Iraq trying to give orders
We need to fix the problems within our own borders.

Chris McDaniel
Grade 8, Standley Middle School
Poet-teacher: Glory Foster
Teacher: Caitlin Cray

WAR

The small town is full of gloom as the train pulls in.
Father and friends get on as the soft snow pours
  down harder.
My eyes begin to water as I recognize this will be the
last time I see him 'til it is over.

The soldiers all pack their guns onto their packs.
We all cry—tall, small, old, young. Soon, the steam
  shoots out
of the train. The wheels begin to turn and soon,
  they are
out of sight. This is the last time.

One winter later, the same train returns half-full,
but then we see Father.

Kyle Rigg
Grade 7, Lewis Middle School
Poet-teacher: Gabriela Anaya Valdepeña
Teacher: Chris Silvestri

Dog Tags of a Fallen Hero
by Brandon Schlegel / Marston Middle School

LOOK AT THAT RUNNER

Bang! Shot out like a bullet,
Combustable, total confidence.
Watch him as he reels the runners in,
Lip jiggling, wind blowing in his face,
Rapid legs, swift arms,
Gliding on the turf,
He throws his head forward,
1st place!

Bashir Wyatt
Grade 6, Montgomery Academy
Poet-teacher: Roxanne Kilbourne
Teacher: V. C. Groves

A Winning Pair by Timothy Tigno / Morse High School

What I am Aiming For

My hands, nestled in leather gloves
  one on my bow
  the other on the string.
I pull back the arrow
  softly, steadily
  but with strength
      like a convict pulling the bars of his cell apart
      trying for freedom.
My hands stop.
I take a breath
  and I wonder
  what I'm aiming for
but I do not know.
I loose the arrow.
  It flies like a rifle shot
  glimmering in the sunlight
  a fiery streak
  across the sky.
It strikes the center of the target
  but I still do not know
      what I am aiming for.

Weslie Hawkins
Grade 8, Standley Middle School
Poet-teacher: Glory Foster
Teacher: Reissa Schrager-Cole

LOVE'S LANGUAGE

A Two-faced World by Brianna Felion / Rose Elementary School

THE WORDS OF RED

Red
Roses on the mountains
Waving with the wind
Sunset in the meadow
Beneath a waterfall
Hot sauce on a plate of spaghetti
At winter time
The swift-changing colors of a chameleon
Blending into the leaves of autumn
The hatred of a friend
Betrayed

Nuria Cruz
Grade 4, John Muir Alternative School
Poet-teacher: Roxanne Kilbourne
Teacher: Marcia Sorini

GIVING TO YOU

I will give you a memory. I will give you the memory of seeing the sun dip into the ocean and submerge to become a nightlight for all fish. I will give you the memory of seeing the moon gather the stars to herself, to see the moon's smudged face peer down to earth to govern our night. I will give you an example of friendship by holding you accountable for your actions, for correcting your mistakes with love, and encouraging you. I will give you the last bit of thread shaven from the last lamb that roamed the wild. I will give you a swimsuit so you can swim in a creek with me and see wonders of the Creator. I will give you the sight of oak trees dressed in their brightest colors in Autumn. I will give you a Band-Aid to put over a puncture wound I accidentally gave you with a pencil. I will give you dessert by secretly eating your salmon for you. I will give you my world and my life for you to do your work through. I will give you my love, as long as I'm alive to love you.

Anna Najor
Grade 7, Heritage Christian School
Poet-teacher: Jill Moses
Teacher: Mary Jane Najor

LA NOVIA

inspired by Julio Galan

La novia walks
Around the church floors
Waiting for the groom
She waits patiently
For him to come
While a child holds her long golden veil
Like a strip of yellowish-silk blanket
Roses and churches are caught
In the netting
She has a blindfold over her eyes
What can't she see?
Did she throw the bouquet in the air
And just catch the holder?
Did she touch the churches
And make them small?
Is this just her imagination
Playing tricks on her?
No, she is in a special place
In Heaven where she belongs
In a blue azure sky.

Lisett Peña
Grade 5, Rose Elementary School
Poet-teacher: Glory Foster
Teacher: Susan McKeon

THE HEART POEM

If I were your heart
I would give you love
lots of hugs
and all the warm tea
you could ever want.

Sarai Velazco
Grade 4, Otay Elementary School
Poet-teacher: Johnnierenee Nelson
Teacher: Carola Pandeli

The Blind Can See Too by Kimberly Garcia / Morse High School

My Perfect Pet

Inside my heart is my gray hamster
trying to run away

Her fur feels like snowflakes
she grins like a saber tooth tiger

Her teeth, sharp as glass
swift lightning

When I call her name
she stands up
as straight as a stick

Alvin Balmeo
Grade 4, Las Palmas Elementary School
Poet-teacher: Johnnierenee Nelson
Teacher: Ida Gordon

Clifford by Jennifer Alfaro / Mann Middle School

THE SOLID DOG WITH LOTS OF FRIENDS

There was once a dog who was very solid
when people crashed into her.

She was a Jewish dog
and her favorite time of year was Hanukkah.
Hanukkah is eight days of only presents.

Her favorite colors were pink, purple and light blue
and she *hated* black.

This dog had five really good friends,
but only two she confided in.

One day she and her friends decided
to have a picnic in the park.

She called her friends and told each one
to bring a different thing
but made sure they didn't bring liver and onions.
They hated liver and onions.

Everyday at the park
they would see a lady picking up dog poop.
They would laugh because they felt so bad.

They always played a game called bouncy;
you have to bounce the ball
and say "BOUNCY BOUNCING."

She loved her family, her friends and God
very much,
but she hated boys in level 5 of dog school.

Alison Tradonsky
Grade 5, San Diego Jewish Academy
Poet-teacher: Jim Milner
Teacher: Cheryl Kolker

Family Portrait

My mother is a wind chime
busily twinkling and clinking
to and fro in the afternoon breeze
an Italian cuisine - zesty, spicy and full of characters
bursting with comedy, always spirited
like a southern chapel on Sunday morning
When she laughs it thunders and pierces
like a nail being driven into the wall
you can feel her pain, her joy, her inspiration
My mother is a breath of moist, fresh air

My father is a new battery always
charged with energy
prepared to complete his job
He is a bowl of gumbo
a Louisiana specialty filled with old cajun charm
He is my shield, my form of fatherly protection
My father is my teacher, a guide to life outside my home

I am a blanket - warm, understanding
logical of the world around me
I am a pair of glasses
intellectual, observant, skeptical
I am time, while slowly ticking, patient
awaiting any event to occur
But at times I move quickly
as fast as a cheetah in the African Savannah
I am light, I guide
I'm a leader, I give new inspiration
to those lost like small children
abandoned in a thunderous storm
I am life, and this is my family portrait

Octavia Marks
Grade 10, Morse High School
Poet-teacher: Johnnierenee Nelson
Teacher: Carol Zupkas

Mi Papá

Papá, todavía me acuerdo
cuando sonaba la alarma en la
mañana, te cambiabas de ropa y
abrías la puerta. Mi Mamá se
levantaba y hacía el café y yo
te lo llevaba. Desayunábamos
y nos llevabas a lugares
o a veces nos llevabas a pasear
al parque con las bicicletas.
Casi cada día nos llevabas comida.
Todavía me acuerdo
cuando te vestías de Santa Clos.
Todavía me acuerdo.

Carla Torres
Grade 4, Euclid Elementary School
Poet-teacher and translator: Francisco Bustos
Teacher: Aida Hernandez

My Father

Father, I still remember
when the alarm would sound in the
morning, you would change clothes
and open the door. Mom would
get up and make coffee, and I
would take it to you. We'd eat breakfast
and you would take us to places
or sometimes you would take us
to ride bicycles at the park.
Almost every day you'd take us food.
I still remember
when you would dress like Santa Claus.
I still remember.

THE OMEN

It belonged to no one
It was lonely and forgotten
My mom's hard working days were long
She washed dishes
Cleaned kitchens
Washed laundry
Cleaning a lady's house
For four months she carried me
An unknown gender
My mom walked under the shady tall trees
Every afternoon
Rested at times on the green grass by the sidewalk
It was there she found it
It was small
Fit in the palm of her hand
Wearing a lime green dress
With teary brown eyes
And a healthy pink-cheeked smile
Which made my mom smile
It was a tiny porcelain doll
She knew what it meant
I was a girl
Her baby girl
It has been 14 years
Since she found the porcelain doll
It's in a special place in my mom's room
Sometimes lonely and forgotten
But greatly remembered
It is a tiny doll
A doll representing my life

Jessica Rodriguez
Grade 8, Standley Middle School
Poet-teacher: Glory Foster
Teacher: Reissa Schrager-Cole

My UCLA Helmet

My UCLA football helmet
is as gold as the sun.
It shines and sparkles
like the biggest star in the universe.
It's hard and ready for everything.
It makes me feel like Junior Taylor
jumping over a pile of people
making a one-handed catch in the end zone.
My helmet takes me back into UCLA history
when my dad had someone fly a plane
over the Rose Bowl during the game and write

"Susan, (my mom) will you marry me?"
while he was sitting next to her.

Morgan Heck
Grade 3, Jerabek Elementary School
Poet-Teacher: Celia Sigmon
Teacher: Ellen Warren

Good-bye by Michelle Hanley / Morse High School

Jackhammer Hands

My dad's hands
wrinkled raisins
rougher than a bully's bite
a rock trying to scratch you.

When he washes his hands
they feel soft
like a swallow's feather
or a bunny's back.

His hands work hard
like jackhammers
breaking up the sidewalk.

Pedro Cardenas
Grade 4, Las Palmas School
Poet-teacher: Johnnierenee Nelson
Teacher: Catherine Pfizenmaier

Poetry's Actions

Poetry,
The comforting outlet of emotions
Where you can ride the color of your soul,
Or the unbreakable wall
Of a Writer's Block.

Sometimes my brain shouts,
"No! Horrible! Not at all!"
Wall after wall,
Appearning,
Barring my flow of thoughts,
And marooning me
On the lifeless
Island of the Unknown.

Yet sometimes,
Sometimes,
A poem comes out as quickly and easily
As a yoyo can fall.
And reading my poem again,
I recapture the feeling of my passion
And catch my shining yoyo of pride.

Kyle Ingraham
Grade 5, Hawthorne Elementary School
Poet-teacher: Veronica Cunningham
Teacher: Tricia Smith

BROWN SCARRED HANDS

My father's hands
Are very rough and big
They are brown and scarred
They work very hard
From 5:30 in the morning
Till 4:30 in the afternoon
They work at construction
Whether it is hot or cold
To put food on the table
And a roof over our heads
His hands pray for others
They help with my homework
By teaching me
His hands rest
After a long day at work
Even though his hands are rough
They leave a warm soft feeling
His hands are like tools
That can build and fix things
Even healing people's hearts

Alejandra Ruiz
Grade 8, Marston Middle School
Poet-teacher: Glory Foster
Teacher: Brandi Swanson

MY FATHER'S HANDS

My father's hands are skinny and pink
with many creases and short nails
and has a white ring around his finger from his
  wedding band.
His hands are very strong and smooth.

He sometimes squeezes my hand or turns a knob.
He opens the record drawer
and turns the lock so no one will peek.

When nervous, dad wrings his hands.
If he clasps his hands then stay out of his way,
  he's angry!
Drumming fingers mean he's bored.
And he high-fives when happy.

He touches my face in love.
He makes the best charoset
on the morning of Pesach.
Always a birthday cake for mom.
He lights the Menorah,
builds the Sukkah,
puts on the talit and kipah.
He holds a siddur,
and a pointer for the torah.

I love my father and his hands.

Dani Shapiro
Grade 5, San Diego Jewish Academy
Poet-teacher: Jim Milner
Teacher: Fran Miller

A WELDER'S HANDS

My Uncle Dale's welding hands
busted-open knuckles
as if he slammed them into a spike bed.

The metal inside
looks like little dimes
squeezed into every slot.

I ask " What are you doing?"
He responds "Making a silver heart for you."

Rikki Jean Celiceo
Grade 5, Otay Elementary School
Poet-teacher: Johnnierenee Nelson
Teacher: Teresa Ledezma-Ruan

A Welder's Hands by Rikki Jean Celiceo / Otay Elementary School

How to Paint Love

Love is the simple
Thing in the most
Complex universe.
It is like the open wing on
The brassy plains.
The grace of a ballerina
Performing her hardest.
It's like the deep night sky
With no moon.
The sadness of the river flowing.
The calm of the ocean with no waves.
It is like the purity
Of the girl you desire
Without her knowing.

Silviano Valdez
Grade 8, Harborside School
Poet-teacher: Jill Moses
Teacher: Kristine Nellis

Ballad of the Orphaned Boy

Sad and cold he waited there
as the wicked rain
fell upon the lonely stair
that lead to the house of pain.

So many times he had cried
as Mother received fierce blows.
Once again his father lied,
more his lies shall grow.

He remembered back to that awful night
his father drunk on ale,
soon his mother's soul took flight.
Sweet Mama was so pale.

He cradled her in the trembling arm
that his father broke.
She tried to protect her boy from harm,
but instead she was choked.

The boy cried harder at the thought
and he tried to forget
how hard his mother had fought
against the who father let

shots bring the boy's sister down.
An orphan he's become.
Mom and Sis sleep in the ground.
His father on the run.

A month has passed since that night
when all this did arise.
So now he writes these poems of loss
to shrink the hate inside.

Sarah Faxon
Grade 8, Marston Middle School
Poet-teacher: Gabriela Anaya Valdepeña
Teacher: Carol Matori

Mirrorless by Ken Lilly / Morse High School

Insomnia by Bannersee Astudillo / Morse High School

DEPRESSED (DRAMATIC POEM)

The fields less green, the apples sour. What I would
give to have you back, Mother! If only you had not
been accused of witchery and burned at the
wretched stake! If you were here, I would love you
like the morning sun, it would have been my
greatest pleasure. Not a friend have I, except for
you. Now you have passed— it's like life without
light, like the cat without it's meow, like the
swallow without day, or nightingale without night.
I have no feeling, no emotion, no aura, no love. I
feel nothing, see nothing but an endless tunnel.
I am but eight, and eight I will stay— now to visit
you for eternity—I throw myself in the flames.

Matthew Higgins
Grade 5, Santa Fe Montessori School
Poet-teacher: Gabriela Anaya Valdepeña
Teacher: Christine Beausoleil

WHAT DO I THINK OF POETRY?

I loathe poetry!
Poetry stinks like rotten onions,
1-year-old sweaty gym socks,
A tank of fuming gasoline,
Unlike enjoyable subjects such as brain-teasing math
  or hands-on science,
Full of fun puzzles and unexpected blasts.

Writing rhymes and rhythms makes my head spin,
And writing about love and romance just makes me
  cringe.
Hey, wait a minute,
I've finished this poem,
It wasn't so bad,
I had fun being witty and using my brain,
I didn't have to use mushy words as I thought I might,
So, maybe poetry is not so bad after all!

Natalie Diebold
Grade 6, Marshall Middle School
Poet-teacher: Veronica Cunningham
Teacher: Deborah Whitehurst

SLOW COOKING

Long Days at Imperial by Jessa Balcita / Morse High School

A CHILD

A child with a storm in her pocket.
Two ogres, mean and naughty—I'm
wishing to grow, wishing for a door
out. Adults with many choices . . .
To Pluto. . . No school! No limit!
Gravity. No tax. No worries. Take me
away.

Sarah LaBanc
Grade 4, Miramar Ranch Elementary School
Poet-teacher: Gabriela Anaya Valdepeña
Teacher: Deborah Hartke

THE BONES ON THE FLOOR

When I eat a poem
It's gonna taste like
A six dollar burger with guacamole
At the place with the star
It would act like a rib plate
All the sauce in my mouth
With bones on the floor
I'd spit out the onion
But keep everything else

Want to know how
You can eat a Dream?

Carlos Sanchez
Grade 4, Rose Elementary School
Poet-teacher: Glory Foster
Teacher: Daina Putnam

SPAGHETTI

Strings of verses
Chewy round balls of stanzas
No need to set any table
No need for any silverware
Slurping up the long lengths
Of infinite words
Like the thick threads
Of a spider's sticky web
And the balls of meat as high as stars
Climbing atop
It looks like Mars
Sauce flowing down all around this sphere
Washing away my competitors
I want to eat it now and here
Eating it without a core
But suddenly I'm on the bottom
Sandwiched between
This giant ball of meat
That I cannot eat

Brian Tran
Grade 8, Marston Middle School
Poet-teacher: Glory Foster
Teacher: Linda Ponsford

Leaves Aren't Perfect by Reizha Ancho / Morse High School

SEA OF WRITING

Letters splash onto
a blank tree.
A branch gracefully skates
across a page
of screaming words.

Andrey Payne
Grade 5, Hawthorne Elementary School
Poet-teacher: Veronica Cunningham
Teacher: Tricia Smith

HOW TO BAKE A POEM

Step 1: Make your poem from scratch or use store bought poems.

Step 2: Take your poem out from your mind.

Step 3: Place it in the oven until crisp with imagination.

Step 4: Remove poem. Sprinkle with icing to make it sweeter for the brain to digest.

Step 5: Begin eating by eating slowly devouring the outer shell to get the essence of your poem.

Step 6: Start making your way towards the center, your poem is becoming softer and gooier.

Step 7: Now you have reached the inner core. It is warm and tender with an unforgettably sweet smell. Don't bother cleaning up, keep your poem around as long as you can so you can soak in its glory.

Jake Rappoport
Grade 8, Standley Middle School
Poet-teacher: Glory Foster
Teacher: Reissa Schrager-Cole

MY FORK IS READY

I love to watch Mom cooking
Tortillas are frying
Chicken spreads across the tortilla
All white meat is
The way we all like it
Mom puts on the cheese
Sprinkling it like fairy dust
The sauce is dark red
Yet on the tortilla
It's lighter
Like the sun coming up
The stove is hot, so are the pans
Cheese melting
Food on the table
Ready to eat
My fork is ready
And so am I
I take a bite
So delicious
We're having enchiladas
At the family table
Mom's kitchen is a shooting star
You never know
What cooking will explode next

Jessica Strickland
Grade 8, Marston Middle School
Poet-teacher: Glory Foster
Teacher: Susan Riddell

The Awakening

Burning toast spewing black smoke,
Bacon bleeding a thick sweat,
Ringing bell syrup micro waved,
Rubbing the green goo from my eyes
Blinking and massaging messy hair,
Pajama pants no shirt or socks,
Scratched plate with leftover crumbs from dinner,
Cups with chewed edges around the top,
Baby crying in highchair,
The start of another great day.

Chris Mancillas
Grade 11, Carlsbad High School
Poet-teacher: Jill Moses
Teacher: Andie Clarke

The Muffinator by Catrina Dulay / Morse High School

Key of Z Confusion

Confusion is
a frog that slithers like a snake
a ballerina shaped like a mermaid
or a piano with only two keys
a jasmine flower with no fragrance

Confusion is
a turtle with no shell
a quesadilla with no cheese
love without a heart

Fernanda Lezama
Grade 7, Marston Middle School
Poet-teacher: Johnnierenee Nelson
Teacher: Jennifer Huerta

KITCHEN IN CHINA

My mom's kitchen is
A rectangular shaped room full of clean windows.
The windows shine of wax and expensive soap.
Plastic roses lounge on the window pane.
Red cherry wood cupboards
Smell like rice cakes.
The tin kettle is a bronze sun.
The food of the last dinner floats in the air
Bacon, rice, eggplant toss,
Strawberry cake, blue and purple cookies
All made in this saintly room
The kitchen in China.
Chopsticks and napkins lie around
Some worn, some brand new.
China plates clattering
The buzz of the range
The sweet smile of Mom
All seep through the door.
The hot air of food fills the kitchen
The makings of white rice and potato stew.
A square window overlooks the street
Where I play tag with my buddies.
The Chinese Kitchen, a place of loving memories.

Sarah Cheng
Grade 8, Standley Middle School
Poet-teacher: Glory Foster
Teacher: Caitlin Cray

China Girl by Tram Pham / Rose Elementary School

LIKE GUM STUCK TO YOUR SHOE

My sister
Hops all around like popcorn
Loud as an alarm
Every where I go
My sister follows
Like gum stuck to your shoe.
Still I love my sister
Like I love money
And take care of her
Like she was my life.
She grows like a tree
Glowing and green
That's my little sister.

Giselle Luevano
Grade 7, Mann Middle School
Poet-teacher: Glory Foster
Teacher: Gail Phillips

CHAMOMILE

Many long years old, the scent of chamomile
fills my senses and memories flow.
My mother's warm lap as a young child,
the sip of warm tea into her mouth.
The peace in the evening air,
as the light bounced off of the walls.
My brothers gathered in the lit den,
the echo of the television
filled my ears.
My mother, a shield against the shadows of the night,
silence filled me,
and my eyes shut to a peaceful slumber.

Mollie Friedlander
Grade 6, Del Mar Heights Middle School
Poet-teacher: Jill Moses
Teacher: Kelly Johnson

RED CARDINALS IN SUMMER

Red is like a sweet strawberry on a hot day,
A flaming fire,
Red cardinal singing in summer,
Blood in my mouth when I fight.
Red is like apple pie with twelve bright cherries on top.

Luis Santos
Grade 6, Montgomery Academy
Poet-teacher: Roxanne Kilbourne
Teacher: V. C. Groves

So This is What Happiness Feels Like
by Erin Pablo / Morse High School

Banana Smoothie

Yellow is sunshine on a summer morning in California
The lemon scent in a white kitchen
The glow of stars
The sky the moment before the sun disappears

Yellow is a banana smoothie on the boardwalk
Cool lemonade being sold at a stand on a suburb corner
Like the citrus sting of oranges and grapefruits
Like a tropical burst of an open flower

Yellow is bright and smiling
Forgiveness and apologies

Yellow is the golden hair of a beach-worn surfer
A forgotten friend
And the reminder of her tears

Siobhan Matheson
Grade 8, John Muir Alternative School
Poet-teacher: Roxanne Kilbourne
Teacher: Amy Masuda

Tiffany the Tangerine Tiger

taught tap dancing
to her friend Teresa the toucan.
The two of them teamed up for a TV show.
Two times a year they would get tattoos.

On Tuesdays, Teresa would
tease Tiffany on the telephone.
On Thursdays, Tiffany would
tickle Teresa while Teresa
pulled Tiffany's tail.

Tiffany Hernandez Diaz
Grade 3, Marshall Elementary School
Poet-teacher: Johnnierenee Nelson
Teacher: Tara Malm

THE FREEZER

My secret hiding place
is in my freezer
    cold as an ice-skating rink
I go there when I'm bored.

When I come out
I smell like catfish.

I stay in there
for five minutes
until I'm calm.

Jimmy Nguyen
Grade 3, Marshall Elementary School
Poet-teacher: Johnnierenee Nelson
Teacher: Tara Malm

Peace Poem

Peace is like a possum scurrying down the road
Peace is like the toad jumping into the water

Peace is like the dolphin swimming in the sea
Peace is like a dog getting a flea off its back

Peace is like a human adopting a puppy
Peace is like a bird getting ready to sing

Peace is like a cat getting down from a tree
Peace is like a mouse getting free from a trap

Peace is like a bear waking up from a long sleep
Peace is like a rabbit digging a deep hole

Peace is like a ferret getting away from a poacher
Peace is like a deer sleeping from a long day

Nick M. Nasirpour
Grade 4, Santa Fe Montessori School
Poet-teacher: Gabriela Anaya Valdepeña
Teacher: Christine Beausoleil

THE OCEAN INSIDE ME

Inside me
There is an ocean.
When I'm angry
Its tides crash violently.
When I'm sad
It flows quietly, dark and gray.
When I'm happy
Its water glistens
And its small tides gently
Reach for the shores of my soul.
When I'm calm
It shines and sleeps.
Inside me
There is an ocean,
Always a mystery.

Christine Kim
Grade 8, Mann Middle School
Poet-teacher: Glory Foster
Teacher: Karen Jackson

Sailing by Jennabel Javier / Morse High School

BLUE POETRY

My bunny eats paper. The beautiful sunshine shines
  on my paper.
I see God move in my poetry. I like blue in my poetry.
My poetry shines like green grass.
My poetry writes words without using a pen.
My poetry shines like a ticket. My poetry looks like an
  eye.
I can see the universe in my poetry. My poetry tastes
  like the world.

Vanessa Chappins
Kindergarten, St. Patrick's School
Poet-teacher: Jill Moses
Teacher: Mary Meyer

HONORABLE MENTIONS

Bright Night by Alejandra Robinson / Longfellow School

HONORABLE MENTIONS

Lonliness by Jezer Balangcod / Morse High School

Ada Harris Elementary School

Jordan Rae Clift, *From Me to You*
Kianna Eberle, *Look at Me*
Tamzin Elliot, *A Moment in Time*
Katherine Joplin, *Awakening* and *Demons*
Crystal Micelli, *Spinning Circles*
Silvia Ramirez, *My Special Rock*
Anniel Ramos, *I Will Give You My Dreams*

Carlsbad High School

Liana Franciosa, *Paint the Occasion*
Tristan Haggard, *Ode to Odes*
Sierra Lam, *Fresh Love*
Erik Mann, *Bitter School*
Mike Mayaudon, *Mango Mirror*

Central Elementary School
Yaritza Alcazar, *Fluffy Hands*
Luis Paz, *Apple* and *Soft Hands*

Charter School of San Diego School

Kevin Hahnlein, *We Are Family*
Adam Khan, *Questions of Contentment*
Quais Sakwall, *A Corrupted Land*

Del Mar Heights Elementary School

Jacqueline Lo, *Ode to an Ice Cube*
Chelsea Mumma, *Fox*
Haru Sakurai, *How to Paint the Future*
Adam Skinner, *Ode to Guga My Dog*

Dingeman Elementary School

John Lee, *Magical Tools of Truth*
Josephine Sheu, *World of Hope and Harmony*

Doyle Elementary School

Nhi Cong Thao Nguyen, *A Surprise Gift*
Angie Wang Shu, *The God of Polished Rocks*

The Giraffe by Kristiana Riego de Dios / Longfellow School

Euclid Elementary School

Candy Alonso, *If I Were the Loving Moon*
Alex Alubaidi, *If I Were Yellow*
Amy Cruz, *Pretty Spring*
Oliver Luvianos, *Mom*
Ramiro Martinez, *Spring*
Deyanira Pelayo, *Spring Is*
Michelle Ros, *It's Springtime*
Wuilvian Segura, *Lo que mi Maestra es para Mi*
Tajjahnee Williams, *If I Was a Velveteen Rabitt*

Flying Hills Elementary School

Jillian N. Jones, *Targets*

Harborside School

Taylor Abram, *Faces in the Wind*
Alison Conover, *Outside and Inside*
Jean-Claude Futterman, *Ode to My DVD Player*
Hunter J. Holthaus, *In the Picture*
Nubbia Mercado, *The Palm Tree Speaks*
Cloe Moctezuma, *Ode to Family Photos*
Elisa Palacios, *Inside Drew's Future*
Genny Riber, *Grey Bridge*
Victoria Valdes, *Ode to the Mango Tree*

Hawthorne Elementary School

Priya Bisarya, *The Waves of the Sea*
Chase Connell, *The Soul's Journey Through Life*
Sarah Herrmann, *Death, Who Are You?*
Max Needham, *The Writing Ball* and *Waking Up*
Angelika Santa-Domingo, *Laughter's Magic*
Channing Tullio, *Forgiveness of the Heart*
Michael Wayne, *The Horrible Headache*
Karly Nicole Zlatic, *Sweet Mother Earth*

Lost by Chelsea Shelton / Marston Middle School

Hearst Elementary School

Alex Adelman, *Walking*
Taryn Boley, *My Mother's Hands*
Celestine Christensen, *Classroom*
Cheyenne Nelson, *Fall Days*
Pravin Wilkins, *Rainy Day*

Heritage Christian School

Alyxandra Barbeau, *Ocean*
Katherine Najor, *You Can Receive*
Zachary O'Brien, *Ode to the Night Sky*
Michelle Peltz, *Silence*

Jerabek Elementary School

Doug E. Barnett, *The Last Storm*
Kaylee Burns, *My Imagination*
Alison Compton, *Slow Night*
Amy Gallagher, *The Moon Frog*
Cal Griencewic, *A New Life*
Chris Hall, *Fall*
Stephen Jacob, *Indian Feather Headband*

Tree of Music by Monica Gallardo / Longfellow School

Camila Kcomt, *The Colors of Fall*
Andy Kim, *My Brother Kevin*
Kendal Krawl, *Dream Night*
Rogan McDaniel, *The Cruel Night*
Ryan Merrill, *A Fall Day*
Ryan Moelter, *Owl in the Night*
Brandon Morse, *Blue is Music*
Taylor Nemanich, *Black is Nothing to Me*
Maria Oljaca, *The Heart*
Shendl Singer, *I've Got the Blues*
Robin Smith, *Magic Bag*
Willy Summers, *The Night Snake*
Brian Tunnell, *Window of Life*
Siobhan Webb, *Night Ghost*
Sarah Weinstein, *The Sun*
Ali Wolman, *It's Snowing*
Allison Zohn, *The Night Creature*

John Muir Alternative School

Brent Englehart, *Fires of Love*

Kearny High School

Jorge Madueño, *Ode to the 619*
Ana Morales, *Liberty in the Sky*

Kimball Elementary School

Judith Cortez, *Chavelita*
Alejandra Reyes Martinez, *My Aunt*
Karina Mendoza, *My Great Grandfather Tata*

La Jolla High School

Marina Olevsky, *Jaded Cynosure*
Hiromi Ueyoshi, *Black Raven*

Las Palmas Elementary School

Ariana Aranas, *Instruments*
Stephen Poutoa, *The World's Hands*
Jasserin Roranes, *Watermelon Hands*
Eduardo Ruiz, *My Mom's Hard-working Hands*
Chelsey Jenna Sanchez, *Ode to the Moon*

Lewis Middle School

Nancy Lee, *La Jolla Bees*
Samantha Morrow, *Ode to My Pool*
Amanda Olson, *Mimosa*
Tawny Protas, *Dance*
Chris Vann, *Hummingbird*

Distraction Twenty-four by Vincent Tan-Torres / Morse High School

Broken Equation by Camille Adonga / Morse High School

Longfellow School
Shaniqua Bates, *Dreams*

Mann Middle School
Jazzmon Lankford, *Metal, Strawberries & Death*
Andrea McCorley, *King David and a Whole Lot of Red*
Timothy Siriphone, *The Green Flying Sheep*
Amanda Starke, *The Siren's Song*

Marshall Elementary School
Carolina Nuñez, *The Hole of My Imagination*

Marshall Middle School
Diana Rae DeBolt, *The Selfish Stories of the Rain*
Megan Elrod, *Oh, the Darkness of the Rain*
Samantha Summers, *The Rain in My Spirit*
Kevin Young, *Writing*

Marston Middle School
Kaylee Anderson, *The Cabin*
Aniruddh Bose-Raut, *A Magpie's Feather*
Jeremy Dewhurst, *Tears*
Mitchell Dodge, *Saturday Night*
Gözde Gültoprak, *Dream of Salty Waves*
Madelline Hohmann, *Sea Life*
Anthony Johnson II, *I See You*
Shuhei Kadoya, *Unfair*

Tonya Keno, *Knitting Butterflies*
Krista Larson, *Of White Doves*
Margerie Lopez, *Like My Heart*
Celene Marin, *Ballad of Marcos*
Ashley Montero, *The Flag*
Paige Nicolet, *A Storm's Beginning*
Laura Ortiz, *Ode to the 99 Cents Store*
Leela Ottombrino, *Deep Beneath the Water's Surface*
Isabel Perez, *Mi Amor Se Fue*
Namphong Pham, *Blind Madness*
Emilio Rivera, *Fiery Revenge*
Alan Sackrider, *Red Silence*
Michelle Sanchez, *Pink*
Natasha Stewart, *Turtles*
Cecilia Uzarraga, *On My Knees*
Shasta Linda Valdez, *The Loneliness of Purple Daisies*
Alex Yong, *The Giver of Dreams*

Miramar Ranch Elementary School

Jennifer Allison, *The Earth*
Erika Lukasik, *Abigail*
Ross J. Miller, *Brown*

Montgomery Academy

Gael Ermac, *Summer Days*
Wicky Inthavong, *Midnight's Freedom*
Shayne Kelley, *Hatred's Shadow*
Danh Le, *Blue My Color*
Daniel Melton, *Weather Man*
Breanna Stovall, *Calmness of Blue*
Bobby Vannasy, *The Evil, the Calm*

Morse High School

Aaron Ayala, *I Paint a Backward Picture*
Mikael Cabal, *Where Do These Stairs Lead?*
Hazel Cruz, *Gritty Guitar Beats*

Jobeth DeVera, *The Dancer Within*
Catrina Dulay, *Corduroy Jacket*
Janice Esteban, *Bulls-eye Hardships*
Elaine R. Fainas, *Painting My Universe*
Czarina Galac, *A Moment in the Snow*
Erica Hunt, *Exposing Locked Doors*
Kay Tiomico Langit, *An Afternoon Delight*
Dung Nguyen, *Bloodline*
Chynna Obana, *Horse-driven Personality*
Suzanne Ogot, *Yippee! It's a Jamboree!*
Marites Ordoñez, *The Olden Days*
Naomi Tamashiro, *Broken But Loving*

Otay Elementary School

Luis Bustillos, *Shimmering Dog*
Lisbeth Machado, *The Pianist's Hands*
Zaira Ramirez, *Violin Like Velvet*

Pacific Beach Elementary School

Nicole Remsburg, *Alive Hope*
Lauren Victor, *Life's Wanderer*

Ramona High School

Matt Blase, *Batman's Revenge*
Kassondra Snyder, *Happiness Is*

Cheerleading Lady by Briana Markham / Rose Elementary School

Rose Elementary School

William Alonzo, *If I Were a Ferrari*
Daniel Anderson, *Glorious Green*
Jesus Castillo, *V is a Vast Village*
Arturo Cazarez, *A Tuatara King*
Jasmine Dominguez, *Butterfly*
Christian Henderson, *A River Journey*
Jaquelin Hernandez, *Joyful J*
Kevin Hua, *T is a Turtle*
Kiyoshi George Kakazu, *Just a Whisper Passing By*
Sammy Kohler, *My Crazy Backyard Jungle*
David Losacco, *Big Jupiter and Little Pluto*
Luke Parker, *The Tornado of the Savannah*
Luis Perez, *Ode to the Oregon Agate*

San Diego Jewish Academy

Emily Beaver, *Paintbrush*
Samantha Kucinski, *The Barn*
Rouen Reouveni, *Colors of My Life*
Katie Sherman, *Love*
Channa Zlotnick, *The Beach*

San Pasqual Union School

Abigail Brown, *Horses of Many Colors*
Elliott Daniel, *The Beauty of the Woodlands*
Jennifer Gorham, *In the House of Love and Life*
Athena Mann, *Pink*
Hailey Neveu, *Pink Pigs*

Santa Fe Montessori School

Ophélie Lavoie-Gagné, *Sadness*

Spreckels Elementary School

Amelia B. Jacobs, *Bats*
Alex Wells, *Zion*

St. Patrick's School

Cole Altemus, *The Color Gold*
Kaden Arkeder, *I Am Everywhere*
Conner Clay Arnold, *The Rock Paper*
Michaelle Burbank, *I Am a Yellow Swan*
Sean Devins, *My Warm Rock*
Megan Fogelstrom, *I'll Give You*
John Gallagher, *The Weather Mask*
Anthony Garibay, *Red, My Favorite Color*
Tess Herzog, *All Poetry That Tess Wrote*
Paige Kelly, *Everything is Different*
Cassondra King, *The Eye of Gold*
Bridget Krol, *The Nature of Me*
Ryan Little, *I Am the Purple Snake*
Emily Ray, *The Red Dog*
Mary Grace Sumner, *I Give You*
Jimmy Zatrine, *Brother*

Standley Middle School

Andy Dunable, *Ode to Summer*
Alexander M. Javier, *Starlight Visitation*

Sunset View Elementary School

Erica Malachowski, *Burning Rain*
Claire Olmstead, *Hidden Treasure*

University City High School

Easton Connell, *The Price is Right*

Paradise by Jimmy Vu / Mann Middle School

Pieces by Rayna Kilroy / Morse High School